T0302028

THE ZACK FILES™

Through the Medicine
Cabinet

I'd like to thank my editors,
Jane O'Connor and Judy Donnelly,
who make the process of writing and revising
so much fun, and without whom
these books would not exist.

I also want to thank
Jennifer Dussling and Laura Driscoll
for their terrific ideas.

Through the Medicine Cabinet

Text copyright © 1996 by Dan Greenburg.
Illustration copyright © 1996 by Jack E. Davis.
All rights reserved.

First published in the United States by Grosset & Dunlap, Inc., a member of Penguin Putnam Books for
Young Readers under the title THROUGH THE MEDICINE CABINET.

This Korean and English edition was published by Longtail Books, Inc. in 2020 by arrangement with
Sheldon Fogelman Agency, Inc. through KCC(Korea Copyright Center Inc.), Seoul.

ISBN 979-11-93992-35-7 14740

Longtail Books

THE ZACK FILES™

Through the Medicine Cabinet

by Dan Greenburg
Illustrated by Jack E. Davis

Long tail Books

For Judith, and for the real Zack,

with love—D.G.

Chapter 1

I'm what you'd call a pretty normal
kid. My name is Zack, which is a pretty
normal name. I'm ten years old, which is
a pretty normal age. I have normal brown
hair and eyes. I have **slight**ly **crook**ed
teeth, which is normal at my age. And I
live in a big apartment building in New
York. I always *thought* my building was

normal, at least until the thing I'm **about to** tell you happened.

I've got to admit I've always been interested in **weird stuff**. Stuff like dead people **crawl**ing out of their **grave**s at night. Or guys who **stare** at you and then suddenly their heads **explode**. I haven't actually seen those things. But who am I to say they couldn't happen?

Anyway, the time I want to tell you about happened at the beginning of spring vacation. My dad **arrange**d to take me down to Florida. We were going to visit the New York Yankees[1] at their spring training[2] **camp**.

---

1 **New York Yankees** 뉴욕 양키스. 1901년에 창단되었으며, 뉴욕을 연고지로 하는 미국 메이저리그 소속의 프로 야구팀.

My parents are **divorce**d. Part of the time I live with my dad. He's a writer, and he gets to do lots of cool things. Like go to spring training and then write about it in a magazine. I can't believe he gets paid to do this stuff. Neither can he.

Saturday morning was when we were planning to leave. I was so excited, I woke up at about 6:00 A.M. The minute I opened my eyes, I **realize**d something. I had forgotten to put my **retainer** in my mouth before I went to sleep. Where the heck[3] was it?

A retainer, **in case** you don't know,

---

2 **spring training** 이른 봄에 스포츠 팀 전체가 기후가 온난한 외국이나 다른 지방에서 하는 훈련.

3 heck '도대체', '젠장' 또는 '제기랄'이라는 뜻으로 당혹스럽거나 짜증스러운 감정을 강조하는 속어.

is **brace**s that you wear on your teeth at night. I don't **exact**ly love my retainer. It's made of **wire** and pink plastic. It's really **gross**-looking, especially when you take it out and put it on the table at lunch.

My dad hates when I lose my retainer. They cost twelve hundred dollars, I think. Or a hundred and twelve. I forget which.

I left one retainer in a pair of jeans, which went in the **laundry**. It **melt**ed to the inside of the pocket. One got **chew**ed up in my Grandma Leah's **garbage disposal**. Another got **flush**ed down the **toilet**. Another one I'm almost **positive** a **rob**ber **stole** while I was out of my room, although I've never been able to **prove** this.

All in all, I have not lost more than

seven of them. Eight, **tops**.

I was sure my retainer was in the **medicine cabinet** in the bathroom, instead of in my mouth, where it should have been. I got up and opened the door of the medicine cabinet. Yes! There was my retainer. But then, just as I was about to close the cabinet door, something weird happened. Something very weird. The back of the medicine cabinet opened. And there, staring right in my face, was a boy who looked almost exactly like me!

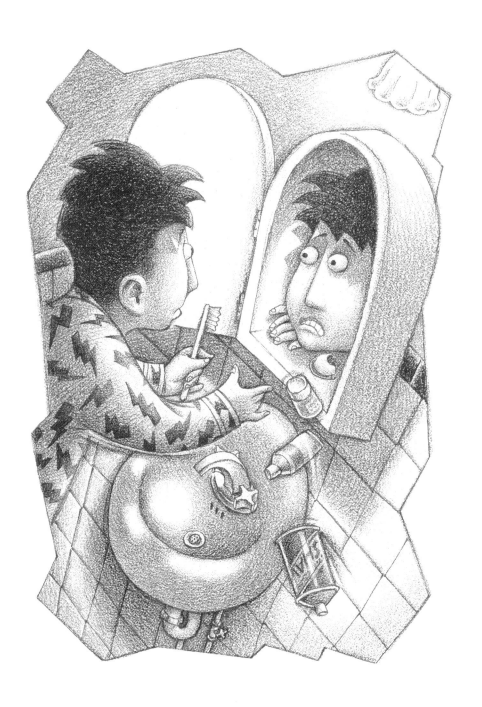

Chapter 2

A boy who looked just like me? How could that be? I was so **startle**d, I **knock**ed over my **retainer**. It fell into his bathroom. Then we both screamed and **slam**med our **medicine cabinet** doors shut.

What the heck was happening here?

Very slowly I opened the medicine cabinet again. Nope. There was nobody on the other side. I pushed against the back of it. It didn't open. Very **weird**.

So where was my retainer? I **figure**d I'd better **check out** the apartment next door. An old lady named Mrs. Taradash lives there.

Mrs. Taradash is kind of **cranky**. I know she isn't too happy about the basketball **hoop** I have **mount**ed on my wall. She's **complain**ed to my dad lots of times. When I slam-dunk,[1] she says it's like a 5.7 **tremor** on the Richter **scale**.[2]

But maybe Mrs. Taradash had a grandson. Maybe her grandson looked almost **exact**ly like me. And maybe her

---

1 **slam-dunk** 슬램 덩크. 농구에서 공중으로 높이 뛰어올라 골대 위에서 공을 강하고 힘차게 내리꽂는 숏.

2 Richter scale 리히터 척도. 지진의 규모를 나타내기 위해 미국의 지질 학자 리히터(C. F. Richter)가 제안한 단위로, 기호 M으로 표시한다.

medicine cabinet was **hook**ed **up** to ours on the other side.

I knew this explanation didn't **make** much **sense**. But it was all I could **come up with**.

I got dressed. Then I **slip**ped quietly out of our apartment. I knocked on Mrs. Taradash's door. There was no answer. I knocked again. It took a while before somebody opened it. Mrs. Taradash was in a **fuzzy robe** and fuzzy **slipper**s. Her hair was all **mess**ed **up**. And she was **rub**bing her eyes. She didn't seem all that **thrill**ed to see me, if you want to know the truth.

"I'm sorry to **bother** you, Mrs. Taradash," I said. "I was wondering whether I could get my retainer out of your bathroom."

"Your what, **precious**?" she said.

She calls all kids "precious." But you can tell she doesn't think they are.

"My retainer," I said.

"What **in the name of heaven** is that, precious?"

"A retainer is **brace**s made out of **wire** and pink plastic, which sometimes falls down **disposal**s or **toilet**s," I explained. "Mine fell into your apartment when your grandson opened the medicine cabinet door."

Mrs. Taradash looked at me like I was **cuckoo**.

"I don't have a grandson, precious," she said.

"You don't have a grandson? Then who opened the other side of my medicine cabinet just now?"

The bottom half of her face smiled. But the top half was **frown**ing. It looked like both halves were fighting with each other. She tried to close the door on my foot.

"Please don't close the door, Mrs. Taradash," I **begg**ed her. "I lost my retainer in your apartment. It's the eighth one that's **gotten away** from me. Maybe the ninth. If I don't get it back, my dad will kill me. You wouldn't want that on your **conscience**, would you?"

She opened the door and looked at me.

"What do you want?" she said. It was more **hiss**ing than talking. And she seemed to have forgotten the word "precious."

"Just my retainer," I said, "which the

boy who's not your grandson will tell you fell into your bathroom from my medicine cabinet. Please just let me look for it."

"If I let you look," she said, "will you go away and let me get back to sleep?"

"Yes, ma'am," I said.

She **sigh**ed a deep sigh. Then she **wave**d me into the apartment.

I went in.

Weird. Everywhere you looked, there were **stuff**ed animals. And I don't mean **cuddly** teddy bears,[3] either. I mean real dead animals that were stuffed by a taxidermist.[4] **Squirrel**s, rabbits, beavers,[5]

---

3 **teddy bear** 테디 베어. 장난감 곰 인형으로, 미국의 26대 대통령 테어도어 루스벨트(Theodore Roosevelt)의 애칭을 따서 만들었다.

4 taxidermist 박제사. 동물의 가죽을 벗기고 썩지 않게 한 뒤에 솜이나 대팻밥 등을 넣어 살아 있는 것처럼 만드는 박제 기술을 가진 사람.

chipmunks.[6] They were all **frozen** in weird **pose**s. And they **stared** at you through their **beady** glass eyes. They really gave me the **creep**s.

I hurried into the bathroom and looked around. There was no retainer on the floor or anywhere else. I opened the medicine cabinet. I pushed against the back. It didn't **budge**. So I closed the medicine cabinet door.

"**Satisfied**?" she hissed.

I had a sudden feeling that if I didn't leave, her eyes would start **glow**ing red. Then she'd **grab** me and try to stuff me.

---

5 **beaver** 비버. 뒷발에 물갈퀴가 발달되어 헤엄을 잘 치는 동물로, 강 등에 댐을 만드는 것으로 유명하다.

6 chipmunk 얼룩 다람쥐. 북미 대륙에서 주로 발견되는 작은 설치류로 몸에 난 줄무늬가 특징이다.

There I'd be, standing **alongside** the other animals in a weird frozen pose, staring at visitors through beady glass eyes.

I **apologize**d and **hotfoot**ed **it** back to my dad's apartment. I didn't have a **clue** what had happened. I began to think I'd dreamed the whole thing. But if I did, then where was my retainer?

On the way back to my bedroom, I passed my bathroom. **Out of the corner of my eye** I thought I saw something.

My medicine cabinet door.

It was slowly creeping open.

Chapter 3

I **race**d into my bathroom. I **yank**ed open the door of the medicine cabinet all the way.

There he was! The same boy I'd seen before.

"Hey!" I said.

He didn't **slam** the door this time. I think he was too **stun**ned. He kept **staring**.

I was staring too. He really did look a whole lot like me. Only his teeth were a lot more **crook**ed.

"Who are you?" I asked.

"Zeke," he said.

"I'm Zack."

"I know."

"You don't live next door," I said. "Do you?"

He shook his head.

"Then where do you live?"

"Someplace else. Someplace **nearby**, but kind of far away, too. Someplace you might think is weird."

"You live in New Jersey?[1]"

---

1 **New Jersey** 뉴저지주(州). 미국 동북부에 위치한 주로 섬유, 금속, 조선 등의 공업이 발달하였다.

He shook his head.

"Then where?"

"Have you ever heard of Newer York?" he said.

"Is that up near Poughkeepsie?[2]" I asked.

He **sigh**ed and **roll**ed **his eyes** like I had just said the stupidest thing in the world. I had a sudden thought.

"Hey," I said, "is this something really weird that I'm going to be sorry I got myself **involve**d in?"

"I have time for just one more question," he said. "And then I have to go."

"OK," I said. "Do you have my retainer?

---

2 **Poughkeepsie** 포킵시. 미국 뉴욕주(州)에 있는 도시로 뉴욕시보다 조금 더 북쪽에 있다.

I think it fell on your side."

He suddenly tried to slam the door. But I was too fast for him. I stuck my arm into the medicine cabinet. That stopped him from shutting it. He **grab**bed my hand and tried to **pry** it off the door. I grabbed his **wrist**.

"Let go!" he shouted.

"Not till you give me my retainer!"

He tried to pull away. I held on tight. He backed up. I hung on with both hands. He pulled me through the medicine cabinet. Then we both fell onto the floor in his bathroom.

"Now you've done it!" he shouted. "Now you've really done it!" He looked **frighten**ed.

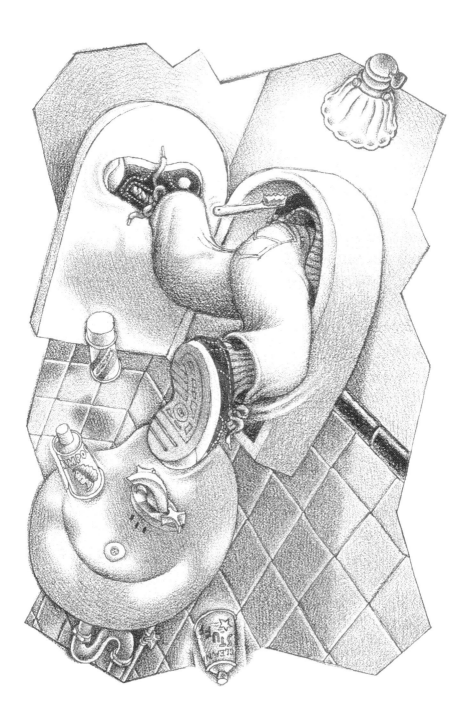

"Done what?" I asked.

"The one thing nobody **is** ever **supposed to** do," he said.

"What's that?" I asked.

"Cross over into a **parallel universe!**[3]"

---

3 **parallel universe** 평행 우주. 공상 과학 소설이나 영화 등에서 사용하는 표현으로, 자신이 살고 있는 세계가 아닌 평행선 상에 위치한 또 다른 세계를 가리킨다.

Chapter 4

"**W**hat the heck is a **parallel universe**?" I asked.

Zeke looked around **nervous**ly.

"Shhhh!" he shouted. "Somebody might hear you!"

"You're the one who's shouting," I said. "What the heck is a parallel universe?"

"Well, it's kind of like this," said Zeke.

"Our universe is right next to yours. It's so close you wouldn't believe it. It even **takes up** some of the same space as yours. Only you can't usually see us. **Except** on **Opening** Days. Like today."

"Today isn't Opening Day," I said. "The baseball season doesn't start for a couple months yet."

Zeke **sigh**ed and shook his head.

"The kind of Opening Day I'm talking about," he said, "has nothing to do with baseball. It's when your universe and mine move right next to each other. It doesn't happen a lot. It'll be years before it happens again."

"Sort of like an eclipse?[1]" I asked.

"Sort of," he said. "When it's Opening

Day, we can look through certain openings, like a **medicine cabinet**. Then we can see your universe. Which, by the way, isn't any better than ours."

"I didn't say it was better," I said. "Did I say it was better?"

"Maybe not. But I **bet** that's what you were thinking," he said. "We've got everything you've got. And it's just as good, believe me. Maybe even better."

"OK, OK!" I said. Then I **pick**ed **myself up** off the floor. I got my first good look at the parallel universe in Zeke's bathroom.

Hmmmm.

---

1 **eclipse** 식(蝕). 한 천체가 다른 천체에 의하여 완전히 또는 부분적으로 가려지는 현상. 달이 지구의 그림자에 가려지는 것을 월식, 태양이 달에 가려지는 것을 일식이라고 한다.

It looked pretty much the same as mine. Only different. First of all, there was something **odd** about the **sink**. There were two **faucet**s. But they were **mark**ed Cold and Not So Cold.

Then I looked at the roll of **toilet** paper by the toilet. It looked like sandpaper.[2] I hoped I wouldn't be in the parallel universe long enough to have to use the bathroom.

I **notice**d there was a lot of water on the floor. When I **glance**d at the shower I saw why. Instead of a shower curtain, there were venetian **blind**s.[3]

---

2 sandpaper 사포(沙布). 유리 가루 등을 발라 붙인 천이나 종이. 물체의 겉면을 문질러서 반들반들하게 만드는 데 사용한다.

3 venetian blind 베니션 블라인드. 얇고 좁은 판을 일정한 간격으로 엮고 늘어뜨려 햇빛을 가리는 블라인드로, 통풍이 잘 된다.

"So what's Newer York like?" I asked.

"**Outstanding**," he said.

"How many channels do you get on TV?" I asked.

He looked at me **suspicious**ly.

"You get more than one channel?" he asked.

"**Never mind**," I said.

"Hey," he said. "Everything in the Big Banana is as good as anything you've got in New York."

"Oh, you call Newer York the Big Banana," I said. "Like we call New York the Big Apple.[4]"

"Bananas are a lot cooler fruit than

---

4 **Big Apple** 뉴욕시의 별명.

apples," he said.

"Look," I said, "I'm sure everything in your universe is every bit as cool as ours, OK? Now can I have my **retainer**? And then will you please help me cross back over?"

"Zeke, are you **pack**ing?" The voice sounded a lot like my dad's.

"Yeah, Dad!" Zeke called back.

"Well, hurry up! The **cab** is coming at 8:00."

I looked at Zeke strangely.

"You're going somewhere with your dad?" I asked.

"Yeah. We have to catch a plane."

I got a sudden **dizzy** feeling.

"Your dad isn't **by any chance** taking

you to the training **camp** of the New York Yankees, is he?" I asked.

"No."

"Well, *that's* a **relief**," I said.

"He's taking me to the training camp of the Newer York Yunkees. They're a **triple**-A minor **league**[5] team. But they're just as good as the Yankees."

"Oh my gosh," I said softly. "Your life is just the same as mine, except a little different, isn't it?"

"Well, duh!" he said. "That's what a parallel universe is, Zack." He sounded like he was talking to a fourth-**grade**r. I

---

5 **triple-A minor league** 북미 프로 야구의 마이너리그는 세부적으로 7개의 등급으로 나뉘는데, 그 가운데 가장 높은 등급의 리그를 말한다.

didn't **appreciate** that, since I happen to be in the fifth grade. "You want to know the truth? I'm a little tired of living in the one that's the copy and not the one that's the **original**."

"You are? But you just said—"

"Never mind what I said. I may live in a parallel universe. But I'm not stupid. Don't you think I'd rather be going to see the Yankees train than the Yunkees?"

"I can't hear you, Zeke!" called his dad. "Are you talking to me?"

"No, to myself!" he shouted. Then to me he said, "Hey, I've got an idea. Why don't we **switch** places? I'll go to the Yankees' training camp with your dad. You can go to the Yunkees' with mine."

"**No way**," I said.

"Never mind," he said. "I didn't want to do it anyway."

"Have you packed your retainer yet?" called Zeke's dad.

"Don't worry about it!" Zeke answered nervously.

"Oh my God," I said. "Don't tell me you can't find your retainer either!"

"So what?" he said.

This was **freak**ing me out.

"Zeke," called his dad. He sounded like he was right outside the door. "Are you in there?"

Zeke looked **scare**d.

"We can't let him see you here," he **whisper**ed. "You've got to hide!"

"Where?"

"Here."

He led me to the **bathtub**. He pulled back the blinds and pushed me inside. Then I heard him open and close the medicine cabinet door. And then nothing. What **was** he **up to**?

I looked at my watch. I had only a half hour before our cab came. What was I doing hiding in a bathtub in a parallel universe? And how was I ever going to get back to mine?

I **peek**ed through the blind. Zeke was nowhere in **sight**. And then I knew.

That little rat[6] had **sneak**ed back

---

6 **rat** '배신자' 또는 '비열한 놈'이라는 뜻의 속어.

through the medicine cabinet door into my
universe!

Chapter 5

I was in a **panic**.

At this very minute, Zeke was pretending to be me. He was getting ready to leave with my dad for the Yankees' training camp in Florida!

I heard a **knock** at the bathroom door.

"Zeke, did you hear me? Are you ready?" said his father's voice.

I **held my breath**.

The door opened. Zeke's father came into the bathroom. Just then I **sneeze**d.

"**Achoo**ooo!"

"Zeke? Are you in the shower?"

"No, sir," I said.

The **blind**s were pulled up. There stood a dad who looked almost **exact**ly like mine.

At first I was **scare**d he might be mad. But then he began to laugh.

"What are you doing in the shower with your clothes on?" he asked.

"Resting," I said.

"There's no time for resting, Zeke. Our **cab** is coming in about half an hour. Have you got your **retainer**? Are you all **pack**ed?"

"Pretty much," I said.

He looked at me **odd**ly and **frown**ed.

"You look a little different, son. Did you **comb** your hair a new way this morning?"

"Yes, sir. I did. That's exactly what I did."

"Uh huh. OK. Well, I still have a few things to do. Zeke, could you run to the dry **cleaner**s quickly and pick up all our cleaning?"

The cleaners! The only place I wanted to go was back through the medicine cabinet. But what could I say?

"Uh, s-sure," I **stammer**ed. "What cleaners would that be again?"

"You know. The one across the street and down the **block**."

"Uh huh. And what block would that

be again?"

He looked at me and raised an **eyebrow**.

"C'mon," he said. "You've gone there lots of times. Just **get going**. We have to leave soon."

"OK," I said.

He handed me a **receipt** and a twenty-dollar **bill**. Then he walked out of the bathroom.

The twenty-dollar bill looked strange. It was **enormous**. And when I **examine**d it closely, I saw that along the top it said "The Un**tied State**s of America." The picture on all the twenty-dollar bills I've seen is of Andrew Jackson.[1] This one was of somebody with **bushy** hair, a **beard**, and nose-glasses.[2] His name was Slappy

Kupperman.

I left the apartment and went down in the elevator. Then I got outside. I wanted to get to the cleaners and back as fast as I could.

At the corner I waited for **traffic** to stop. It was taking forever. Then I looked up at the traffic **signal** and I saw why. Instead of a red and a green light, there were four lights.

The lights said, "STOP," "NOT YET," "**HOLD ON**," and "OK, GO ALREADY."

Newer York sure was a **weird** place.

---

1 **Andrew Jackson** 앤드루 잭슨. 미국의 7대 대통령으로 국민 중심의 정치를 추진하였다는 점에서 높이 평가받지만, 그의 북미 원주민 강제 이주 정책은 많은 비판을 받는다.

2 nose-glasses 코안경. 안경다리가 없이 코에 걸게 만든 안경을 말한다.

A big billboard[3] to my right said, "WE
LOVE NEWER YORK! JUST AS GOOD
AS NEW YORK. MAYBE BETTER!" Well, I
didn't think so. I wanted to get back to my
own universe.

I did manage to find the cleaners. I got
Zeke's dad's clothes. Then I **beat it** out of
there. I went back down the block. But I
must have gotten **mess**ed **up** somehow.
Because when I got to the corner, the big
billboard should have been to my left. But
it wasn't there at all.

I took a quick look around. Nothing
looked **familiar**. Then I saw a big
apartment building across the street. It

---

3 **billboard** 건물 바깥이나 고속 도로변 등에 세운 대형 옥외 광고판.

had a **fancy canopy**. It looked a whole lot like one in my own **neighbor**hood in my own universe. The Beekman Arms Plaza Apartments. I thought maybe the **doorman** could help me find my way back to Zeke's. The problem was, I didn't even know Zeke's stupid address. All I knew was that it would probably be like mine. Only a little different.

I ran to the building. But there wasn't any doorman. In fact, there wasn't even any building! What I thought was a building was only a **fake** front, like a movie set. The **bush**es in front of it were made of green plastic. There was a **tag** on them. It said, "**Realistic** bushes. **Last** longer. Need less care. Better than real."

I **gulp**ed. I felt like I was in a dream. One of those really **awful** ones where, **no matter how** hard you try to get someplace, you can't, and then you **puke**.

In the middle of the street I saw an open **manhole**. There were police **barricade**s around it. **Sign**s said, "DANGER ON **OPENING** DAYS! FALLING IN WOULD BE STUPID! ALSO **PAINFUL**! DID WE **MENTION ILLEGAL**?"

Hey! This could be another way to get back to my universe! If I couldn't find my way back to Zeke's and go through the medicine cabinet, maybe I could climb through here. Going through the **sewer**s would be pretty **gross**, of course. But I didn't care. At least I'd come out on the right side.

I waited for the traffic light to change. Again it took forever. Then I **race**d up to the manhole. Now was the time to make my move. But just as I **stoop**ed down, I felt a heavy hand on my shoulder.

I looked up. A big policeman was standing over me. He seemed kind of **scary**. But then I looked at the gun in his **holster**. It was a Super **Soaker**.[4]

"You wouldn't want to get too close and fall into New York," he said. "Now would you, sonny?"

"Oh boy,[5] sir. I sure wouldn't want to

---

4 **Super Soaker** 물을 쏘아 보내며 가지고 노는 장난감 물총 가운데 하나.
5 boy 여기에서는 '소년'이라는 뜻이 아니라, '맙소사!' 또는 '어머나!'라는 의미로 놀람이나 실망, 기쁨 등을 나타내는 표현으로 쓰였다.

do that," I said.

We both laughed pretty hard at the idea I'd want to do anything as stupid as fall into New York.

"Well then, step away from there," he said.

I did. He stayed right next to the manhole. I don't think he trusted me. But with his Super Soaker he didn't seem so scary anymore. I decided to ask his help.

"Um, **Officer**," I said, "I'm kind of lost. I was on my way home. But I must have taken a wrong turn or something."

"What's your address, son?" he asked.

"My address?"

"Yes."

"Uh, well, I'm not exactly sure," I said. "I

mean it seems to have **temporarily slip**ped my mind."

"Your address has slipped your mind?"

"Temporarily."

He looked at me strangely. But he listened while I described Zeke's building.

"Oh, I know the one you mean," he said. "I'll take you there."

He took me by the hand. Then he led me down the block and around the corner.

There it was, Zeke's building! I thanked him **all over the place**, and then I **took off**. He was probably glad to **get rid of** me.

Right in front of Zeke's building was a **newsstand**. It was just like the one in front of my own building. On the **front page** of all the newspapers were big **headline**s:

"DANGER! OPENING DAY ARRIVES! CITIZENS WARNED NOT TO **TAKE CHANCES!**"

Danger? What danger? I picked up a paper and started to read.

"Today, in the early hours of the morning, citizens of Newer York will once again be able to **peek** through any of several openings and actually **observe** life in our sister universe. 'Do not **attempt** to cross over into the **alternate** universe!' warns Professor Roland Fenster at the Newer York **Institute** of Parallel Universes. 'The openings should appear somewhere in the **vicinity** of 6:00 A.M. They will then shut down tight again **approximate**ly two hours later. Once shut, they will not

reopen for as many as thirty years. Thirty years would be one heck of a long time to spend in a universe that's **rumor**ed to be better than ours, but isn't.'"

I looked at my watch. **Yikes!** It was 7:45 A.M. I had just fifteen minutes before the cab came and Zeke left for Florida with my dad. And before the doors to my universe **slam**med shut for thirty years!

I raced into Zeke's building.

Chapter 6

arrived back in Zeke's apartment **out of breath**. I dropped Zeke's dad's cleaning in the **hallway**. I **race**d into the bathroom.

I pushed hard against the back of the **medicine cabinet**. But I couldn't make the darned[1] thing **budge**. Zeke **obvious**ly

---

1 **darned** 말하는 내용을 강조하기 위해 덧붙이는 속어로 '젠장맞을' 또는 '빌어먹을'이라는 뜻이다.

knew more about traveling between **universe**s than I did!

And then I heard somebody behind me. I **whirl**ed around to find Zeke's dad looking at me strangely.

"Zeke," he said, "what are you doing?"

Should I tell him the truth? Could I trust him? Or was he the **enemy**? I didn't know. But time was **run**ning **out**. And I didn't see that I had much choice.

"Listen, sir," I said, "this is going to sound sort of **incredible**. But it's the truth, so help me."

"All right, Zeke," he said. "But make it fast. We have less than fifteen minutes before the cab comes."

"OK," I said. "First of all, I'm not your

son, Zeke. I'm somebody else who looks just like him. And my name is Zack. I live in the **parallel** universe. My dad and I were getting ready to go to the Yankees' training **camp**. Just like you and Zeke were getting ready to go to the Yunkees' training camp. Only I dropped my **retainer** through the medicine cabinet. I lost it, the same as Zeke lost his."

Zeke's dad's mouth dropped open. He **smack**ed his **forehead** with his hand.

"I can't be-lieve it!" he said.

"It's true, though, sir," I said. "I **swear**."

"Zeke has lost his retainer?" he said in a **daze**d voice. "That's the tenth one so far this year."

Wow! Zeke was even worse than me!

"Do you know how much those things cost?" he asked.

"Either twelve hundred dollars or a hundred and twelve dollars," I said quickly. "But didn't you hear the other **stuff** I told you?"

"Yes, yes, yes. Of course I did," he said. "Your name is Zack. You live in the parallel universe on the other side of the medicine cabinet, **blah**, blah, blah."

"You don't believe me, do you?" I said.

"Why shouldn't I believe you?" he said. "Everybody in Newer York knows about your universe. It's not like it's a big secret or anything. And it isn't any better than ours either, by the way."

Boy, this was a **touchy subject** with

these guys!

"I never said it was better," I said.
"Look, sir, you seem to know a lot about
parallel universes. So maybe you know
how to **slip** back through the medicine
cabinet to mine. Like Zeke did just now."

"Zeke?" he said. "He crossed over?"

I **nod**ded. I really had Zeke's dad's
attention now.

"But it's almost 7:50!" Zeke's dad
smacked his forehead again. "At 8:00
Opening Day will shut down **complete**ly!"

"My point **exact**ly, sir," I said. "I'd be
miserable if that happened. Not that I
wouldn't love living here, I mean. Because
I think it's at least as good as my universe.
And maybe even better. But the thing is,

I'd really miss my mom and dad."

"OK, OK," said Zeke's dad. "This is what you have to do. Put your hand on the back wall of the medicine cabinet."

I did.

"Close your eyes. Take a deep breath. Now **visualize** the back wall opening. Let me know if you feel anything."

I did everything he said. It started to work. The wall was starting to feel kind of **springy**. I opened my eyes **in time** to see it sort of **melt** away.

Chapter 7

"Hi, Zack," said a **familiar** face.

"Zeke!" said Zeke's dad. "Oh, **thank heavens!**"

"Zeke!" I said. "Were you coming back?"

He looked **embarrass**ed.

"I got **homesick**," he said. "I mean, your dad is **awful**ly nice, Zack. He really is. But he's not my dad. And this isn't my

universe. I **figure**d you must feel the same way. Even though Newer York is just as cool as New York."

My dad appeared on the other side of the **medicine cabinet**.

"Dad!" I said.

"Hi, Zack," said my dad. Then he turned to Zeke's dad. "Hi, Don," he said. "Long time, no see."

"Hi, Dan," said Zeke's dad to my dad.

They shook hands through the medicine cabinet.

"You two *know* each other?" I asked, **amaze**d.

"Yeah, we met when we were your age," said Zeke's dad. "But it wasn't through a medicine cabinet. It was through

a dryer in the **laundromat**."

"Yeah," said my dad. "I always wondered what happened to **odd** socks that got lost in the **laundry**. Who'd have guessed they go to the **parallel** universe?"

"That was quite an **Opening** Day," said Zeke's dad. "Not much laundry got dried. But we sure had fun. Your dad thought I lived in the dryer."

Both my dad and Zeke's dad started **laughing their heads off**.

"Uh, excuse me for **interrupt**ing," I said. "This is all very interesting. But it's now 7:55."

"Oh, right, right!" said Zeke's dad. He looked through the cabinet at Zeke. "Do you still want to go to the Yunkees' training **camp**, son?"

"I sure do!" said Zeke.

"Then let me pull you through," said Zeke's dad.

So Zeke **crawl**ed back into his own universe. I crawled back into mine.

"I'm sorry, Zack," said Zeke. "I was a real **jerk**."

"You were," I said. "But I forgive you."

Cab horns were now **honk**ing on both sides of the cabinet.

"Well, **so long**, guys," I said.

"See you again sometime," said Zeke.

"Maybe at the next Opening Day," I said.

"OK," said Zeke.

He **fish**ed something **out** of his pocket.

He handed it to me through the cabinet. It was my **retainer**!

"You **swipe**d my retainer?" I said.

He **nod**ded **sheepish**ly.

"But I couldn't keep it," he said.

"Because you knew it was wrong."

"Yeah," he said. "Also, it didn't **fit**."

Then all of a sudden, the grandfather clock[1] in our **hallway** started **chiming**.

It was 8:00.

We **wave**d good-bye to each other. Then, instead of **facing** Zeke and his dad, I was looking at **shelves** with toothpaste and deodorant.[2] I pushed hard against

---

1 **grandfather clock** 대형 괘종시계. 추에 의해 움직이는 진자가 몸체 속에 들어 있는 시계. 시계의 몸체가 크고 바닥에 꼿꼿하게 바로 서 있다.

2 deodorant 땀내나 악취 등을 제거하거나 약하게 하려고 몸에 바르는 제품.

the back wall of the medicine cabinet. I **visualize**d like crazy. But nothing happened.

So that's how I **discover**ed the parallel universe. And every time I open my medicine cabinet, I think of Zeke and his dad. I kind of miss them. It's funny to think that they're so close, and yet so far away.

The next time I see Zeke, I could have a son of my own. **Weird**! I wonder what he'll be like. Hey, wouldn't it be cool if he's just like me? In every way **except** one: I hope he doesn't ever need to wear a retainer!

Through the Medicine Cabinet

by Dan Greenburg
Illustrated by Jack E. Davis

CONTENTS

평범한 소년이 겪는 기상천외하고 흥미로운 모험을 그린 이야기, 잭 파일스!

『잭 파일스(The Zack Files)』 시리즈는 뉴욕에 사는 평범한 소년 잭이 겪는 때로는 으스스하고, 때로는 우스꽝스러운 모험을 담고 있습니다. 저자 댄 그린버그(Dan Greenburg)는 자신의 아들 잭에게서 영감을 받아 그를 주인공으로 한 이야기를 떠올렸고, 잭과 같은 아이들이 독서에 흥미를 갖기를 바라는 마음을 담아 이 책을 썼습니다.

초자연적인 현상에 대한 저자의 관심을 녹여 낸 『잭 파일스』 시리즈는 누구나 한 번쯤은 들어 본 기괴한 이야기들을 아이들이 재미있게 읽을 수 있도록 흥미진진하게 소개하고 있습니다. 현재까지 총 30권의 책이 출간되어 전 세계 아이들의 호기심을 불러일으키고 있으며, 동명의 TV 드라마로도 제작되어 많은 관심과 사랑을 받기도 했습니다.

이러한 이유로 『잭 파일스』 시리즈는 '엄마표 · 아빠표 영어'를 진행하는 부모님과 초보 영어 학습자라면 반드시 읽어야 하는 영어원서로 자리 잡았습니다. 간결한 어휘로 재치 있게 풀어 쓴 이야기는 영어원서가 친숙하지 않은 학습자들에게도 즐거운 원서 읽기 경험을 선사할 것입니다.

번역과 단어장이 포함된 워크북, 그리고 오디오북까지 담긴 풀 패키지!

이 책은 영어원서 『잭 파일스』 시리즈에, 탁월한 학습 효과를 거둘 수 있도록 다양한 콘텐츠를 덧붙인 책입니다.

- 영어원서: 본문에 나온 어려운 어휘에 볼드 처리가 되어 있어 단어를 더욱 분명하게 인지할 수 있고, 문맥에 따른 자연스러운 암기 효과를 얻을 수 있습니다.
- 단어장: 원서에 볼드 처리된 어휘의 의미가 완벽하게 정리되어 있어 사전 없이 원서를 수월하게 읽을 수 있으며, 반복해서 등장하는 단어에 '복습' 표기를 하여 자연스럽게 복습을 돕도록 구성했습니다.
- 번역: 영문과 비교할 수 있도록 직역에 가까운 번역을 담았습니다. 원서 읽기에 익숙하지 않은 초보 학습자도 어려움 없이 내용을 파악할 수 있습니다.
- 퀴즈: 챕터별로 내용을 확인하는 이해력 점검 퀴즈가 들어 있습니다.
- 오디오북: 본문 전체에 대한 오디오북을 포함하고 있어, 듣기 훈련은 물론

소리 내어 읽기에까지 폭넓게 사용할 수 있습니다.

『잭 파일스』, 이렇게 읽어 보세요!

● **단어 암기는 이렇게!** 처음 리딩을 시작하기 전, 오늘 읽을 챕터에 나오는 단어들을 눈으로 쭉 훑어봅니다. 모르는 단어는 좀 더 주의 깊게 보되, 손으로 쓰면서 완벽하게 암기할 필요는 없습니다. 본문을 읽으면서 이 단어를 다시 만나게 되는데, 그 과정에서 단어의 쓰임새와 어감을 자연스럽게 익히게 됩니다. 이렇게 책을 읽은 후에 단어를 다시 한번 복습하세요. 복습할 때는 중요하다고 생각하는 단어들을 손으로 쓰면서 꼼꼼하게 외우는 것도 좋습니다. 이런 방식으로 책을 읽으면 많은 단어를 빠르고 부담 없이 익힐 수 있습니다.

● **리딩할 때는 리딩에만 집중하자!** 원서를 읽는 중간중간 모르는 단어가 나온다고 워크북을 바로 펼쳐 보거나, 곧바로 번역을 찾아보는 것은 크게 도움이 되지 않습니다. 모르는 단어나 이해되지 않는 문장들은 따로 가볍게 표시만 해 두고, 전체적인 맥락을 파악하며 속도감 있게 읽어 나가세요. 리딩을 할 때는 속도에 대한 긴장감을 잃지 않으면서 리딩에만 집중하는 것이 좋습니다. 모르는 단어와 문장은 리딩을 마친 후에 한꺼번에 정리하는 '리뷰' 시간을 통해 점검하는 시간을 가지면 됩니다. 리뷰를 할 때는 번역은 물론 단어장과 사전도 꼼꼼하게 확인하면서 어떤 이유에서 이해가 되지 않았는지 생각해 봅니다.

● **번역 활용은 이렇게!** 이해가 가지 않는 문장은 번역을 통해서 그 의미를 파악할 수 있습니다. 하지만 한국어와 영어는 정확히 1:1 대응이 되지 않기 때문에 번역을 활용하는 데에도 지혜가 필요합니다. 의역이 된 부분까지 억지로 의미를 대응해서 이해하려고 하기보다, 어떻게 그런 의미가 만들어진 것인지 추측하면서 번역은 참고 자료로 활용하는 것이 좋습니다.

● **듣기 훈련은 이렇게!** 리스닝 실력을 향상시키고 싶다면 오디오북을 적극적으로 활용해 보세요. 처음에는 오디오북을 틀어 놓고 눈으로 해당 내용을 따라 읽으면서 훈련을 하고, 이것이 익숙해지면 오디오북만 틀어 놓고 '귀를 통해' 책을 읽어 보세요. 눈으로 읽지 않은 책이라도 귀를 통해 이해할 수 있을 정도가

되면, 이후에 영어 듣기로 어려움을 겪는 일은 거의 없을 것입니다.

- **2~3번 반복해서 읽자!** 영어 초보자라면 처음부터 완벽하게 이해하려고 하는 것보다는 2~3회 반복해서 읽을 것을 추천합니다. 처음 원서를 읽을 때는 생소한 단어들과 스토리 때문에 내용 파악에 급급할 수밖에 없습니다. 하지만 일단 내용을 파악한 후에 다시 읽으면 문장 구조나 어휘의 활용에 더 집중하게 되고, 원서를 더 깊이 있게 읽을 수 있습니다. 그 과정에서 리딩 속도에 탄력이 붙고 리딩 실력 또한 더 확고히 다지게 됩니다.

- **'시리즈'로 꾸준히 읽자!** 한 작가의 책을 시리즈로 읽는 것 또한 영어 실력 향상에 큰 도움이 됩니다. 같은 등장인물이 다시 나오기 때문에 내용 파악이 더 수월할 뿐 아니라, 작가가 사용하는 어휘와 표현들도 반복되기 때문에 탁월한 복습 효과까지 얻을 수 있습니다. 롱테일북스의 『잭 파일스』시리즈는 현재 6권, 총 31,441단어 분량이 출간되어 있습니다. 시리즈를 꾸준히 읽다 보면 영어 실력이 자연스럽게 향상될 것입니다.

원서 본문 구성

내용이 담긴 원서 본문입니다.
원어민이 읽는 일반 원서와 같은 텍스트지만, 암기해야 할 중요 어휘들은 볼드체로 표시되어 있습니다. 이 어휘들은 지금 들고 계신 워크북에 챕터별로 정리되어 있습니다.

학습 심리학 연구 결과에 따르면, 한 단어씩 따로 외우는 단어 암기는 거의 효과가 없다고 합니다. 단어를 제대로 외우기 위해서는 문맥(context) 속에서 단어를 암기해야 하며, 한 단어당 문맥 속에서 15번 이상 마주칠 때 완벽하게 암기할 수 있다고 합니다.

이 책의 본문에서는 중요 어휘를 볼드체로 강조하여, 문맥 속의 단어들을 더 확실히 인지(word cognition in context)하도록 돕고 있습니다. 또한 대부분의 중요 단어들은 다른 챕터에서도 반복해서 등장하기 때문에 이 책을 읽는 것만으로도 자연스럽게 어휘력을 향상시킬 수 있습니다.

본문 하단에는 내용 이해를 돕기 위한 '각주'가 첨가되어 있습니다. 각주는 굳이 암기할 필요는 없지만, 알아 두면 도움이 될 만한 정보를 설명하고 있습니다. 각주를 참고하면 스토리를 더 깊이 있게 이해할 수 있어 원서를 읽는 재미가 배가됩니다.

THE ZACK FILES

워크북(Workbook) 구성

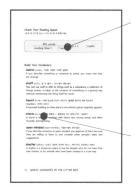

Check Your Reading Speed
해당 챕터의 단어 수가 기록되어 있어, 리딩 속도를 측정할 수 있습니다. 특히 리딩 속도를 중시하는 독자들이 유용하게 사용할 수 있습니다.

Build Your Vocabulary
본문에 볼드 표시되어 있는 단어들이 정리되어 있습니다. 리딩 전·후에 반복해서 보면 원서를 더욱 쉽게 읽을 수 있고, 어휘력도 빠르게 향상될 것입니다.

단어는 〈스펠링 - 빈도 - 발음기호 - 품사 - 한글 뜻 - 영문 뜻〉 순서로 표기되어 있으며 빈도 표시(★)가 많을수록 필수 어휘입니다. 반복해서 등장하는 단어는 빈도 대신 '복습'으로 표기되어 있습니다. 품사는 아래와 같이 표기했습니다.

n. 명사 │ a. 형용사 │ ad. 부사 │ v. 동사
conj. 접속사 │ prep. 전치사 │ int. 감탄사 │idiom 숙어 및 관용구

Comprehension Quiz
간단한 퀴즈를 통해 읽은 내용에 대한 이해력을 점검해 볼 수 있습니다.

한국어 번역
영문과 비교할 수 있도록 최대한 직역에 가까운 번역을 담았습니다.

이 책의 수준과 타깃 독자

- **미국 원어민 기준:** 유치원 ~ 초등학교 저학년
- **한국 학습자 기준:** 초등학교 저학년 ~ 중학생
- 영어원서 완독 경험이 없는 초보 영어 학습자
- **비슷한 수준의 다른 챕터북:** Arthur Chapter Book,* Flat Stanley,* Tales from the Odyssey,* Junie B. Jones,* Magic Tree House, Marvin Redpost

  ★ 「롱테일 에디션」으로 출간된 도서

 QR 코드를 인식하여 「잭 파일스」 2권 원서 오디오북을 들어 보세요! 더불어 롱테일북스 홈페이지(www.longtailbooks.co.kr)에서도 오디오북 MP3 파일을 다운로드 받을 수 있습니다.

Chapter 1

1. **How did Zack use to feel about his apartment building?**

   A. He felt like it was old.

   B. He felt like it was crowded.

   C. He felt like it was unique.

   D. He felt like it was ordinary.

2. **Why was Zack planning to go to Florida?**

   A. To play baseball

   B. To watch a big baseball game

   C. For his dad's work

   D. For a school assignment

3. When did Zack realize he was not wearing his retainer?

A. When he woke up in the morning

B. As he was getting ready for bed

C. When he arrived in Florida

D. As he was packing for his trip

4. What happened to some of Zack's previous retainers?

A. They broke at the dentist's office.

B. They were destroyed by household appliances.

C. They became too small for Zack's teeth.

D. They got eaten by Zack's pets.

5. Why did Zack look for his retainer in the medicine cabinet?

A. It was the only place he had not looked yet.

B. He heard a voice coming from inside it.

C. His dad suggested he check there.

D. He figured it had to be there.

Check Your Reading Speed

1분에 몇 단어를 읽는지 리딩 속도를 측정해보세요.

$$\frac{488 \text{ words}}{\text{reading time ( ) sec}} \times 60 = (\text{) WPM}$$

Build Your Vocabulary

✽ **slight** [slait] a. 약간의, 조금의; 작고 여윈 (slightly ad. 약간, 조금)
Slightly means to some degree but not to a very large degree.

crook [kruk] v. (손가락·팔을) 구부리다; n. 사기꾼, 도둑; 구부러진 곳
(crooked a. 비뚤어진, 구부러진)
If you describe something as crooked, especially something that is usually straight, you mean that it is bent or twisted.

be about to idiom 막 ~하려는 참이다
If you are about to do something, you are going to do it immediately.

＊ **weird** [wiərd] a. 기이한, 기묘한; 기괴한, 섬뜩한
If you describe something or someone as weird, you mean that they are strange.

＊ **stuff** [stʌf] n. 일, 것, 물건; v. 박제하다; 쑤셔 넣다; 채워 넣다
You can use stuff to refer to things such as a substance, a collection of things, events, or ideas, or the contents of something in a general way without mentioning the thing itself by name.

✽ **crawl** [krɔ:l] v. 기어가다; 우글거리다; n. 기어가기
When you crawl, you move forward on your hands and knees.

✽ **grave** [greiv] n. 무덤, 묘; a. 심각한
A grave is a place where a dead person is buried.

stare [stɛər] v. 빤히 쳐다보다, 응시하다; n. 빤히 쳐다보기, 응시
If you stare at someone or something, you look at them for a long time.

explode [iksplóud] v. 폭발하다; 굉음을 내다; 갑자기 ~하다
If an object such as a bomb explodes or if someone or something explodes it, it bursts loudly and with great force, often causing damage or injury.

arrange [əréindʒ] v. 마련하다, 처리하다; 정리하다, 배열하다
If you arrange with someone to do something, you make plans with them to do it.

camp [kæmp] n. (합숙) 캠프; 야영지, 텐트; v. 야영하다 (training camp n. 훈련 캠프)
A training camp for soldiers or sports players is an organized period of training at a particular place.

divorce [divɔ́:rs] v. 이혼하다; n. 이혼, 별거
If a man and woman divorce or if one of them divorces the other, their marriage is legally ended.

realize [rí:əlàiz] v. 깨닫다, 알아차리다; 실현하다, 달성하다
If you realize that something is true, you become aware of that fact or understand it.

retainer [ritéinər] n. 치아 교정 장치
A retainer is a device that you wear in your mouth helps to straighten your teeth.

in case idiom (~할) 경우에 대비해서
If you do something in case or just in case a particular thing happens, you do it because that thing might happen.

brace [breis] n. 치아 교정기; 버팀대; v. (스스로) 대비를 하다; (몸에) 단단히 힘을 주다
A brace is a metal device that can be fastened to a child's teeth in order to help them grow straight.

exact [igzǽkt] a. 정확한; 꼼꼼한, 빈틈없는 (not exactly ad. 전혀 ~이 아닌)
You use not exactly to indicate that a meaning or situation is slightly different from what people think or expect.

☀ **wire** [waiər] n. 철사; 전선; v. 전선을 연결하다; 배선 공사를 하다
A wire is a long thin piece of metal that is used to fasten things or to carry electric current.

⁎ **gross** [grous] a. 역겨운; 아주 무례한; ad. 모두 (합해서)
If you describe something as gross, you think it is very unpleasant.

⁎ **laundry** [lɔ́:ndri] n. 세탁물; 세탁
Laundry is used to refer to clothes, sheets, and towels that are about to be washed, are being washed, or have just been washed.

☀ **melt** [melt] v. 녹다; (감정 등이) 누그러지다; n. 용해
When a solid substance melts or when you melt it, it changes to a liquid, usually because it has been heated.

⁎ **chew** [ʧuː] v. 물어뜯다, 깨물다; (음식을) 씹다; n. 씹기, 깨물기
(chew up idiom 엉망으로 부수다)
If something gets chewed up, it becomes torn apart and destroyed.

⁎ **garbage** [gáːrbidʒ] n. (음식물·휴지 등의) 쓰레기
Garbage is rubbish, especially waste from a kitchen.

☀ **disposal** [dispóuzəl] n. 음식물 쓰레기 처리기; 처리; 처분
A disposal or a garbage disposal is a small machine in the kitchen sink that breaks down waste matter so that it does not block the sink.

⁎ **flush** [flʌʃ] v. (변기의) 물을 내리다; (얼굴이) 붉어지다; n. 홍조
If you flush something down the toilet, you get rid of it by putting it into the toilet bowl and making water pass through the toilet.

⁎ **toilet** [tɔ́ilit] n. 변기; 화장실
A toilet is a large bowl with a seat, or a platform with a hole, which is connected to a water system and which you use when you want to get rid of urine or feces from your body.

☀ **positive** [pázətiv] a. 확신하는; 분명한; 긍정적인
If you are positive about something, you are completely sure about it.

rob [rab] v. (사람·장소를) 도둑질하다 (robber n. 강도)
A robber is someone who steals money or property from a bank, a shop, or a vehicle, often by using force or threats.

steal [stiːl] v. (stole–stolen) 훔치다, 도둑질하다; 살며시 움직이다
If you steal something from someone, you take it away from them without their permission and without intending to return it.

prove [pruːv] v. 입증하다, 증명하다; (~임이) 드러나다
If you prove that something is true, you show by means of argument or evidence that it is definitely true.

all in all idiom 전체적으로, 대체로
You use all in all to introduce a summary or general statement.

tops [taps] ad. 최고로; a. (인기·능력 등이) 최고인, 제1인자인
You can use tops after mentioning a quantity, to say that it is the maximum possible.

medicine [médəsin] n. 약, 약물; 의학, 의술, 의료
Medicine is a substance that you drink or swallow in order to cure an illness.

cabinet [kǽbənit] n. 캐비닛, 보관장; (정부의) 내각
A cabinet is a cupboard used for storing things such as medicine or alcoholic drinks or for displaying decorative things in.

Chapter 2

1. Who did Zack think the boy in the medicine cabinet might be at first?

A. His secret twin

B. Someone related to his neighbor

C. Someone he just imagined

D. A ghost from his neighbor's home

2. What did Mrs. Taradash say to Zack?

A. She was too busy to help.

B. She did not have a grandson.

C. Zack could buy a new retainer.

D. Zack should be more careful with his retainer.

3. Why did Mrs. Taradash let Zack into her home?

   A. So that he would stop bothering her soon

   B. So that no one could hear their conversation

   C. So that they could find the boy together

   D. So that they would be safe from the boy

4. What did Zack notice about Mrs. Taradash's apartment?

   A. It was full of stuffed animals for kids.

   B. It had pictures of animals on display.

   C. It had books on various animals.

   D. It contained actual stuffed animals.

5. What did Zack discover in Mrs. Taradash's bathroom?

   A. There was no medicine cabinet.

   B. The back of the medicine cabinet was missing.

   C. The medicine cabinet was normal.

   D. The retainer in the medicine cabinet was not his.

Check Your Reading Speed

1분에 몇 단어를 읽는지 리딩 속도를 측정해보세요.

$$\frac{759 \ words}{reading \ time \ (\quad) \ sec} \times 60 = (\quad) \ WPM$$

Build Your Vocabulary

⋆ **startle** [stɑːrtl] v. 깜짝 놀라게 하다; 움찔하다; n. 깜짝 놀람 (startled a. 깜짝 놀란)
If something sudden and unexpected startles you, it surprises and frightens you slightly.

⋆ **knock** [nak] v. 부딪치다; (문 등을) 두드리다; n. 문 두드리는 소리; 부딪침
If you knock something, you touch or hit it roughly, especially so that it falls or moves.

복습 **retainer** [ritéinər] n. 치아 교정 장치
A retainer is a device that you wear in your mouth helps to straighten your teeth.

⋆ **slam** [slæm] v. 쾅 닫다; 세게 치다, 놓다; n. 쾅 하고 닫기; 탕 하는 소리
If you slam a door or window or if it slams, it shuts noisily and with great force.

복습 **medicine** [médəsin] n. 약, 약물; 의학, 의술, 의료
Medicine is a substance that you drink or swallow in order to cure an illness.

복습 **cabinet** [kæbənit] n. 캐비닛, 보관장; (정부의) 내각
A cabinet is a cupboard used for storing things such as medicine or alcoholic drinks or for displaying decorative things in.

복습 **weird** [wiərd] a. 기이한, 기묘한; 기괴한, 섬뜩한
If you describe something or someone as weird, you mean that they are strange.

figure [fígjər] v. 생각하다; 중요하다; n. (멀리서 흐릿하게 보이는) 사람; 수치
If you figure that something is the case, you think or guess that it is the case.

check out idiom ~을 확인하다; (흥미로운 것을) 살펴보다
If you check someone or something out, you examine them in order to be certain that everything is correct, true, or satisfactory.

cranky [krǽŋki] a. 성미가 까다로운, 짓궂은; 기이한
Someone who is cranky is not very cheerful and gets angry easily.

hoop [hu:p] n. (농구의) 림; (큰) 테
A basketball hoop is the ring that players try to throw the ball into in order to score points for their team.

mount [maunt] v. 고정시키다; (자전거·말 등에) 올라타다; n. (물건을 세우는) 대; 산
If you mount an object on something, you fix it there firmly.

complain [kəmpléin] v. 불평하다, 항의하다
If you complain about a situation, you say that you are not satisfied with it.

tremor [trémə:r] n. 미진(微震), 진동; (약간의) 떨림
A tremor is a small earthquake.

scale [skeil] n. (측정용) 등급; 규모; 눈금; v. (아주 높고 가파른 곳을) 오르다
A scale is a set of levels or numbers which are used in a particular system of measuring things or are used when comparing things.

exact [igzǽkt] a. 정확한; 꼼꼼한, 빈틈없는 (exactly ad. 정확히)
You use exactly when you emphasize that something is no more and no less than a number or amount, or is completely correct in every detail.

hook up idiom 걸다
If you hook up one thing to another, you attach it there using a hook.

make sense idiom 이해가 되다; 타당하다
If something makes sense, you can understand it.

come up with idiom (아이디어·계획 등을) 생각해내다; (돈을) 마련하다
If you come up with a plan or an idea, you think of it and suggest it.

⁎ **slip** [slip] v. 슬며시 가다; 미끄러지다; n. (작은 종이) 조각; 미끄러짐
If you slip somewhere, you go there quickly and quietly.

fuzzy [fʌ́zi] a. 솜털이 보송보송한; 흐릿한, 어렴풋한; (머리카락이) 곱슬곱슬한
If something is fuzzy, it has a covering that feels soft and like fur.

⁎ **robe** [roub] n. 가운; 예복
A robe is a piece of clothing, usually made of toweling, which people wear in the house, especially when they have just got up or had a bath.

⁎ **slipper** [slípər] n. (pl.) 실내화
Slippers are loose, soft shoes that you wear at home.

mess up idiom ~을 엉망으로 만들다; 혼란스럽게 하다; 실수하다
If you mess up something, you make it untidy or dirty.

⁑ **rub** [rʌb] v. (손·손수건 등으로) 문지르다; (두 손 등을) 맞비비다; n. 문지르기, 비비기
If you rub a part of your body, you move your hand or fingers backward and forward over it while pressing firmly.

⁎ **thrill** [θril] v. 열광시키다, 정말 신나게 하다; n. 흥분, 설렘; 전율 (thrilled a. 아주 신이 난)
If someone is thrilled, they are extremely pleased about something.

⁎ **bother** [báðər] v. 신경 쓰이게 하다, 괴롭히다; 신경 쓰다; n. 성가심
If someone bothers you, they talk to you when you want to be left alone or interrupt you when you are busy.

⁎ **precious** [préʃəs] n. 귀여운 사람; a. 귀중한, 값비싼; 소중한; ad. 정말 거의 없는
Precious is used as a term of address for a beloved person.

in the name of heaven idiom 도대체; 제발
People sometimes use 'in the name of heaven' to add emphasis to a question or request.

brace [breis] n. 치아 교정기; 버팀대; v. (스스로) 대비를 하다; (몸에) 단단히 힘을 주다
A brace is a metal device that can be fastened to a child's teeth in order to help them grow straight.

wire [waiər] n. 철사; 전선; v. 전선을 연결하다; 배선 공사를 하다
A wire is a long thin piece of metal that is used to fasten things or to carry electric current.

disposal [dispóuzəl] n. 음식물 쓰레기 처리기; 처리; 처분
A disposal or a garbage disposal is a small machine in the kitchen sink that breaks down waste matter so that it does not block the sink.

toilet [tɔ́ilit] n. 변기; 화장실
A toilet is a large bowl with a seat, or a platform with a hole, which is connected to a water system and which you use when you want to get rid of urine or faeces from your body.

cuckoo [kúːkuː] a. 미친; n. [동물] 뻐꾸기
If you say that someone is cuckoo, you mean that they are crazy.

frown [fraun] v. 얼굴을 찡그리다; 눈살을 찌푸리다; n. 찡그림, 찌푸림
When someone frowns, their eyebrows become drawn together, because they are annoyed, worried, or puzzled, or because they are concentrating.

beg [beg] v. 간청하다, 애원하다; 구걸하다
If you beg someone to do something, you ask them very anxiously or eagerly to do it.

get away idiom 빠져나가다; 벗어나다
To get away from a person or place means to escape from that person or that place.

conscience [kánʃəns] n. 양심; (양심의) 가책
Your conscience is the part of your mind that tells you whether what you are doing is right or wrong.

hiss [his] v. (화난 어조로) 낮게 말하다; 쉿 하는 소리를 내다; n. 쉭쉭거리는 소리
If you hiss something, you say it forcefully in a whisper.

* **sigh** [sai] v. 한숨을 쉬다, 한숨짓다; 탄식하듯 말하다; n. 한숨
When you sigh, you let out a deep breath, as a way of expressing feelings such as disappointment, tiredness, or pleasure.

‡ **wave** [weiv] v. 손짓하다; (손·팔을) 흔들다; n. 파도, 물결; 흔들기
If you wave someone away or wave them on, you make a movement with your hand to indicate that they should move in a particular direction.

복습 **stuff** [stʌf] v. 박제하다; 쑤셔 넣다; 채워 넣다; n. 일, 것, 물건 (stuffed a. 박제된)
If a dead animal is stuffed, it is filled with a substance so that it can be preserved and displayed.

cuddle [kʌdl] v. (애정 표시로) 껴안다; n. 포옹 (cuddly a. 껴안을 수 있는)
A cuddly toy is soft and designed to be suitable for putting your arms around it.

* **squirrel** [skwə́:rəl] n. [동물] 다람쥐
A squirrel is a small animal with a long furry tail. Squirrels live mainly in trees.

‡ **freeze** [fri:z] v. (froze–frozen) (두려움 등으로 몸이) 굳어지다; 얼다; n. 동결; 한파
(frozen a. 굳어진)
If someone who is moving freezes, they suddenly stop and become completely still and quiet.

* **pose** [pouz] n. 포즈, 자세; v. 자세를 취하다; (위협·문제 등을) 제기하다
A pose is a particular way that you stand, sit, or lie, for example when you are being photographed or painted.

복습 **stare** [stɛər] v. 빤히 쳐다보다, 응시하다; n. 빤히 쳐다보기, 응시
If you stare at someone or something, you look at them for a long time.

beady [bí:di] a. 반짝거리는
Beady eyes are small, round, and bright.

* **creep** [kri:p] n. (pl.) 오싹한 느낌; v. 살금살금 움직이다; 아주 천천히 움직이다
(give the creeps idiom ~를 소름 끼치게 하다)
If someone or something gives you the creeps, they make you feel very nervous or frightened.

budge [bʌdʒ] v. 약간 움직이다, 꼼짝하다; 의견을 바꾸다
If someone or something will not budge, they will not move.

*__satisfied__ [sǽtisfàid] a. 만족하는, 흡족해하는
If you are satisfied with something, you are happy because you have got
what you wanted or needed.

*__glow__ [glou] v. 빛나다, 타다; (얼굴이) 상기되다; n. (은은한) 불빛; 홍조
If something glows, it produces a dull, steady light.

*__grab__ [græb] v. (와락·단단히) 붙잡다; 급히 ~하다; n. 와락 잡아채려고 함
If you grab something, you take it or pick it up suddenly and roughly.

*__alongside__ [əlɔ́ːŋsáid] prep. ~ 옆에, 나란히; ~와 함께; ~와 동시에
If one thing is alongside another thing, the first thing is next to the
second.

*__apologize__ [əpálədʒàiz] v. 사과하다
When you apologize to someone, you say that you are sorry that you
have hurt them or caused trouble for them.

hotfoot it idiom 부리나케 가다, 서둘러 가다
If you hotfoot it, you go somewhere fast and in a hurry.

*__clue__ [kluː] n. 실마리; (범행의) 단서 (do not have a clue idiom 전혀 모르다)
If you do not have a clue about something, you do not know anything
about it or you have no idea what to do about it.

out of the corner of one's eye idiom 곁눈질로; 흘낏 보고
If you see something out of the corner of your eye, you see it but not
clearly because it happens to the side of you.

Chapter
3

1. What did Zeke look like?

A. He looked younger than Zack.

B. He looked dirtier than Zack.

C. His teeth were not as straight as Zack's.

D. His hair was not as neat as Zack's.

2. Where was Zeke from?

A. Someplace cool but unsafe

B. Someplace both weird and fun

C. Someplace small but modern

D. Someplace both close and far away

3. What happened when Zeke tried to shut the cabinet door?

 A. His foot got stuck in it.

 B. Zack prevented him from closing it.

 C. He and Zack broke it off.

 D. He found it was too heavy to move.

4. What was Zack determined to do?

 A. Get his retainer back from Zeke

 B. Find out where Zeke lived

 C. Make Zeke leave him alone

 D. Ask Zeke more personal questions

5. Why was Zeke scared?

 A. His family did not like visitors.

 B. Zack was not allowed in his world.

 C. The floor of his bathroom got damaged.

 D. There was no way Zack could get back home.

Check Your Reading Speed

1분에 몇 단어를 읽는지 리딩 속도를 측정해보세요.

$$\frac{340 \text{ words}}{\text{reading time ( ) sec}} \times 60 = (\quad) \text{ WPM}$$

Build Your Vocabulary

☆ **race** [reis] v. 쏜살같이 가다; 경주하다; n. 경주; 인종
If you race somewhere, you go there as quickly as possible.

yank [jæŋk] v. 홱 잡아당기다; n. 홱 잡아당기기
If you yank someone or something somewhere, you pull them there
suddenly and with a lot of force.

복습 **slam** [slæm] v. 쾅 닫다; 세게 치다, 놓다; n. 쾅 하고 닫기; 탕 하는 소리
If you slam a door or window or if it slams, it shuts noisily and with
great force.

☆ **stun** [stʌn] v. 깜짝 놀라게 하다; 어리벙벙하게 하다; 기절시키다 (stunned a. 깜짝 놀란)
If you are stunned by something, you are extremely shocked or surprised
by it and are therefore unable to speak or do anything.

복습 **stare** [stɛər] v. 빤히 쳐다보다, 응시하다; n. 빤히 쳐다보기, 응시
If you stare at someone or something, you look at them for a long time.

복습 **crook** [kruk] v. (손가락·팔을) 구부리다; n. 사기꾼, 도둑; 구부러진 곳
(crooked a. 비뚤어진, 구부러진)
If you describe something as crooked, especially something that is
usually straight, you mean that it is bent or twisted.

☆ **nearby** [niərbái] a. 인근의, 가까운 곳의; ad. 가까운 곳에
If something is nearby, it is only a short distance away.

ᵇˢsigh [sai] v. 한숨을 쉬다, 한숨짓다; 탄식하듯 말하다; n. 한숨
When you sigh, you let out a deep breath, as a way of expressing feelings such as disappointment, tiredness, or pleasure.

roll one's eyes idiom 눈을 굴리다
If you roll your eyes or if your eyes roll, they move round and upward to show you are bored or annoyed.

⁎involve [inválv] v. 관련시키다, 연루시키다; 수반하다, 포함하다
(get involved in idiom ~에 관여하다, 개입하다)
If you get involved in an activity or event, you take part in it, or you are connected with it in some way.

ᵇˢgrab [græb] v. (와락·단단히) 붙잡다; 급히 ~하다; n. 와락 잡아채려고 함
If you grab something, you take it or pick it up suddenly and roughly.

pry [prai] v. ~을 비틀어 떼어 내다; (사생활을) 캐묻다
If you pry something off or pry it away from a surface, you force it open or away from a surface.

⁎wrist [rist] n. 손목
Your wrist is the part of your body between your hand and your arm which bends when you move your hand.

⁎frighten [fraitn] v. 겁먹게 하다, 놀라게 하다 (frightened a. 겁먹은, 무서워하는)
If you are frightened, you are anxious or afraid, often because of something that has just happened or that you think may happen.

be supposed to idiom ~해야 한다, ~하기로 되어 있다
If you say that something is supposed to happen, you mean that it is planned or expected.

⁎parallel [pǽrəlèl] a. 아주 유사한; 평행한; n. ~와 아주 유사한 것; v. ~와 유사하다
Parallel events or situations happen at the same time as one another, or are similar to one another.

⁎universe [júːnəvəːrs] n. 우주; 은하계; (특정한 유형의) 경험 세계
A universe can be a world or an area of space that is different from the one we are in.

Chapter 4

1. What was true about Opening Day?

A. It had never happened before.

B. It was when Zack and Zeke's universes were farthest apart.

C. It was the only time that Zeke could not be seen.

D. It did not occur frequently.

2. What did Zeke's dad expect Zeke to do?

A. Take a cab to school

B. Get ready to leave their home

C. Go on a tour of the Big Banana

D. Give Zack his retainer back

3. What was Zeke's life like?

A. It was exactly the same as Zack's life.

B. It was the exact opposite of Zack's life.

C. It had huge differences from Zack's life.

D. It had many similarities to Zack's life.

4. Why did Zeke want to switch places with Zack?

A. He wanted to experience original things.

B. He wanted to play a trick on everyone.

C. He wanted to prove his universe was better.

D. He wanted to meet his real dad.

5. Why did Zack hide in the bathtub?

A. So that he could calm himself down

B. So that he could ignore Zeke

C. So that he could give Zeke time to escape

D. So that he could avoid Zeke's dad

Check Your Reading Speed
1분에 몇 단어를 읽는지 리딩 속도를 측정해보세요.

$$\frac{921 \ words}{reading \ time \ (\quad) \ sec} \times 60 = (\qquad) \ WPM$$

Build Your Vocabulary

parallel [pǽrəlèl] a. 아주 유사한; 평행한; n. ~와 아주 유사한 것; v. ~와 유사하다
Parallel events or situations happen at the same time as one another, or are similar to one another.

universe [júːnəvəːrs] n. 우주; 은하계; (특정한 유형의) 경험 세계
A universe can be a world or an area of space that is different from the one we are in.

nervous [nə́ːrvəs] a. 겁내는, 긴장한, 두려워하는 (nervously ad. 초조하게)
If someone is nervous, they are frightened or worried about something that is happening or might happen, and show this in their behavior.

take up idiom (시간·공간을) 차지하다, 쓰다
If something takes up a particular amount of time, space, or effort, it uses that amount.

except [iksépt] prep. (~을) 제외하고는
You use except to introduce the only thing or person that a statement does not apply to, or a fact that prevents a statement from being completely true.

opening [óupəniŋ] n. 구멍, 틈; 개막식; 시작 부분; 공석 (opening day n. 개막식)
An opening is a hole or empty space through which things or people can pass.

sigh [sai] v. 한숨을 쉬다, 한숨짓다; 탄식하듯 말하다; n. 한숨
When you sigh, you let out a deep breath, as a way of expressing feelings such as disappointment, tiredness, or pleasure.

medicine [médəsin] n. 약, 약물; 의학, 의술, 의료
Medicine is a substance that you drink or swallow in order to cure an illness.

cabinet [kǽbənit] n. 캐비닛, 보관장; (정부의) 내각
A cabinet is a cupboard used for storing things such as medicine or alcoholic drinks or for displaying decorative things in.

bet [bet] v. (~이) 틀림없다; (내기 등에) 돈을 걸다; n. 짐작, 추측; 내기
You use expressions such as 'I bet,' 'I'll bet,' and 'you can bet' to indicate that you are sure something is true.

pick oneself up idiom (넘어졌다가) 일어나다; 회복하다
If you pick yourself up, you stand up again after falling.

odd [ad] a. 이상한, 특이한; (신발·양말·장갑 등이) 한 짝만 있는; 홀수의
If you describe someone or something as odd, you think that they are strange or unusual.

sink [siŋk] n. 세면대; 싱크대; v. 가라앉다; 주저앉다; 줄어들다
A sink is a large bowl, usually with taps for hot and cold water, for washing your hands and face.

faucet [fɔ́:sit] n. 수도꼭지
A faucet is a device that controls the flow of a liquid or gas from a pipe or container.

mark [ma:rk] v. 표시하다; 자국을 내다; n. 자국, 흔적
If you mark something with a particular word or symbol, you write that word or symbol on it.

toilet [tɔ́ilit] n. 화장실; 변기 (toilet paper n. (화장실용) 화장지)
Toilet paper is thin soft paper that people use to clean themselves after they have got rid of urine or feces from their body.

ᵗ notice [nóutis] v. 알아채다, 인지하다; 주의하다; n. 신경 씀, 알아챔; 통지, 예고
If you notice something or someone, you become aware of them.

ᵗ glance [glæns] v. 흘깃 보다; 대충 훑어보다; n. 흘깃 봄
If you glance at something or someone, you look at them very quickly
and then look away again immediately.

ᵗ blind [blaind] n. (창문에 치는) 블라인드; v. (잠시) 안 보이게 하다; a. 눈이 먼
A blind is a roll of cloth or paper which you can pull down over a window
as a covering.

ᵗ outstanding [àutstǽndiŋ] a. 매우 좋은, 굉장한; 뛰어난; 두드러진
If you describe someone or something as outstanding, you think that
they are very remarkable and impressive.

ᵗ suspicious [səspíʃəs] a. 의심스러워하는; 의심스러운; 의혹을 갖는
(suspiciously ad. 미심쩍게)
If you are suspicious of someone or something, you do not trust them,
and are careful when dealing with them.

never mind idiom 신경 쓰지 마
You use never mind to tell someone that they need not do something
or worry about something, because it is not important or because you
will do it yourself.

ᵗ retainer [ritéinər] n. 치아 교정 장치
A retainer is a device that you wear in your mouth helps to straighten
your teeth.

ᵗ pack [pæk] v. (짐을) 싸다; 가득 채우다; n. 무리, 집단; 묶음
When you pack a bag, you put clothes and other things into it, because
you are leaving a place or going on holiday.

ᵗ cab [kæb] n. 택시
A cab is a taxi.

ᵗ dizzy [dízi] a. 어지러운; (너무 변화가 심해) 아찔한
If you feel dizzy, you feel that you are losing your balance and are about
to fall.

by any chance idiom 혹시, 혹시라도
You can use by any chance when you are asking questions in order to find out whether something that you think might be true is actually true.

camp [kæmp] n. (합숙) 캠프; 야영지, 텐트; v. 야영하다 (training camp n. 훈련 캠프)
A training camp for soldiers or sports players is an organized period of training at a particular place.

relieve [rilíːv] v. 안도하다; (불쾌감·고통 등을) 없애 주다; 완화하다 (relief n. 안도, 안심)
If you feel a sense of relief, you feel happy because something unpleasant has not happened or is no longer happening.

triple [tripl] a. 3개로 이뤄진; 3배의; v. 3배가 되다
Triple means consisting of three things or parts.

league [liːg] n. (스포츠 경기의) 리그; 연합, 연맹
A league is a group of teams that play the same sport or activity against each other.

grade [greid] n. 학년; (상품의) 품질; 등급; v. (등급을) 나누다; 성적을 매기다
(grader n. 학년생)
Grader combines with words such as 'first' and 'second' to form nouns which refer to a child or young person who is in a particular grade in the American education system.

appreciate [əpríːʃièit] v. 고마워하다; 진가를 알아보다
If you appreciate something that someone has done for you or is going to do for you, you are grateful for it.

original [ərídʒənl] n. 원본; a. 원래의; 독창적인
If something such as a document, a work of art, or a piece of writing is an original, it is not a copy or a later version.

switch [swiʧ] v. 서로 바꾸다; 전환하다, 바꾸다; n. 스위치; 전환
If you switch two things, you replace one with the other.

no way idiom 절대로 안 돼; 말도 안 돼; 싫어
You can say 'no way' as an emphatic way of saying 'no.'

freak [fri:k] v. 기겁하게 하다; n. 괴짜, 괴물; 기이한 일
If someone freaks out or if something freaks them out, they react very strongly to something that shocks, angers, excites or frightens them.

⁑ **scare** [skɛər] v. 놀라게 하다; 무서워하다; n. 불안(감); 놀람, 공포 (scared a. 무서워하는)
If you are scared of someone or something, you are frightened of them.

⁎ **whisper** [hwíspər] v. 속삭이다, 소곤거리다; n. 속삭임, 소곤거리는 소리
When you whisper, you say something very quietly, using your breath rather than your throat, so that only one person can hear you.

bathtub [bǽθtʌb] n. 욕조
A bathtub is a long, usually rectangular container which you fill with water and sit in to wash your body.

be up to idiom (특히 나쁜 짓을) 하고 있다; ~에 달려 있다
To be up to something means to be secretly doing something that you should not be doing.

peek [pi:k] v. (재빨리) 훔쳐보다; 살짝 보이다; n. 엿보기
If you peek at something or someone, you have a quick look at them, often secretly.

⁑ **sight** [sait] n. 시야; 광경, 모습; 보기; 시력; v. 갑자기 보다
If something is in sight or within sight, you can see it.

⁎ **sneak** [sni:k] v. (sneaked/snuck–sneaked/snuck) 살금살금 가다; 몰래 하다;
a. 기습적인
If you sneak somewhere, you go there very quietly on foot, trying to avoid being seen or heard.

Chapter 5

1. **What did Zeke's dad ask Zack?**

    A. He asked if Zack felt sick.

    B. He asked if Zack wanted to take a walk.

    C. He asked Zack to go get their clothes.

    D. He asked Zack to do the laundry.

2. **What did Zack see when he went outside?**

    A. A billboard promoting Newer York

    B. A traffic signal with no lights

    C. Real trees and bushes

    D. The doorman of a fancy apartment building

3. Why did Zack try to go down the manhole?

A. He thought it might be a good hiding place.

B. He thought it might lead him to his universe.

C. He thought it might be a shortcut to Zeke's home.

D. He thought it might take him directly to Zeke.

4. Why did Zack ask the policeman for help?

A. He wanted to report that Zeke was gone.

B. He did not want to accidentally break the law.

C. The policeman looked smart enough to help him.

D. The policeman did not seem threatening to him anymore.

5. What did Zack read in the newspaper?

A. Citizens should stay away from the openings.

B. No one was permitted to enter the openings alone.

C. Exploring the openings was great opportunity.

D. The openings would be open all day.

Check Your Reading Speed

1분에 몇 단어를 읽는지 리딩 속도를 측정해보세요.

$$\frac{1,299 \text{ words}}{\text{reading time (} \quad \text{) sec}} \times 60 = (\quad) \text{ WPM}$$

Build Your Vocabulary

＊panic [pǽnik] n. 극심한 공포, 공황; 허둥지둥함; v. 어쩔 줄 모르다, 공황 상태에 빠지다
Panic is a very strong feeling of anxiety or fear, which makes you act without thinking carefully.

복습 knock [nak] n. 문 두드리는 소리; 부딪침; v. 부딪치다; (문 등을) 두드리다
A knock is the sound of something hard hitting a hard surface.

hold one's breath idiom 숨을 죽이다
If you say that someone is holding their breath, you mean that they are waiting anxiously or excitedly for something to happen.

＊sneeze [sniːz] v. 재채기하다; n. 재채기
When you sneeze, you suddenly take in your breath and then blow it down your nose noisily without being able to stop yourself, for example because you have a cold.

achoo [aːtʃúː] int. 에취 (재채기 하는 소리)
Achoo is used, especially in writing, to represent the sound that you make when you sneeze.

복습 blind [blaind] n. (창문에 치는) 블라인드; v. (잠시) 안 보이게 하다; a. 눈이 먼
A blind is a roll of cloth or paper which you can pull down over a window as a covering.

복습 exact [igzǽkt] a. 정확한; 꼼꼼한, 빈틈없는 (exactly ad. 정확히)
You use exactly when you emphasize that something is no more and no less than a number or amount, or is completely correct in every detail.

scare [skɛər] v. 놀라게 하다; 무서워하다; n. 불안(감); 놀람, 공포 (scared a. 무서워하는)
If you are scared that something unpleasant might happen, you are nervous and worried because you think that it might happen.

cab [kæb] n. 택시
A cab is a taxi.

retainer [ritéinər] n. 치아 교정 장치
A retainer is a device that you wear in your mouth helps to straighten your teeth.

pack [pæk] v. (짐을) 싸다; 가득 채우다; n. 무리, 집단; 묶음
When you pack a bag, you put clothes and other things into it, because you are leaving a place or going on holiday.

odd [ad] a. 이상한, 특이한; (신발·양말·장갑 등이) 한 짝만 있는; 홀수의
(oddly ad. 이상하게)
If you describe someone or something as odd, you think that they are strange or unusual.

frown [fraun] v. 얼굴을 찡그리다; 눈살을 찌푸리다; n. 찡그림, 찌푸림
When someone frowns, their eyebrows become drawn together, because they are annoyed, worried, or puzzled, or because they are concentrating.

* **comb** [koum] v. 빗다, 빗질하다; 샅샅이 찾다; n. 빗; 빗질
When you comb your hair, you tidy it using a comb.

cleaner [klíːnər] n. (= dry cleaners) 세탁소; 청소부
A cleaner or dry cleaners is a shop where things such as clothes are cleaned with a liquid chemical rather than with water.

* **stammer** [stǽmər] v. 말을 더듬다; n. 말 더듬기
If you stammer, you speak with difficulty, hesitating and repeating words or sounds.

block [blak] n. (도로로 나뉘는) 블록, 구역; 사각형 덩어리; v. 막다, 차단하다; 방해하다
A block in a town is an area of land with streets on all its sides.

eyebrow [áibràu] n. 눈썹
Your eyebrows are the lines of hair which grow above your eyes.

get going idiom 가다; 시작하다
When you get going, you start doing something or start a journey, especially after a delay.

receipt [risíːt] n. 영수증; 수령, 인수
A receipt is a piece of paper that you get from someone as proof that they have received money or goods from you.

bill [bil] n. 지폐; 고지서, 청구서; 계산서; v. 청구서를 보내다
A bill is a piece of paper money.

enormous [inɔ́ːrməs] a. 거대한, 막대한
Something that is enormous is extremely large in size or amount.

examine [igzǽmin] v. 자세히 살펴보다, 검사하다; 조사하다
If two things are untied, they are not joined as one and do not have a close connection.

tie [tai] v. 묶다; 매다; 연결시키다 (untied a. 묶이지 않은)
If two things are untied, they are not joined as one and do not have a close connection.

state [steit] n. 주(州); 상태; 국가, 나라; v. 말하다, 진술하다
A state is a part of a large country with its own government, such as in Germany, Australia, or the USA.

bushy [búʃi] a. 숱이 많은; 무성한, 우거진
Bushy hair or fur is very thick.

beard [biərd] n. (턱)수염
A man's beard is the hair that grows on his chin and cheeks.

traffic [trǽfik] n. 차량들, 교통; 수송
Traffic refers to all the vehicles that are moving along the roads in a particular area.

‡ **signal** [sígnəl] n. 신호(등); 징조; v. 신호를 보내다; 암시하다 (traffic signal n. 신호등)
Traffic signals are sets of red, amber, and green lights at the places where roads meet. They control the traffic by signaling when vehicles have to stop and when they can go.

hold on idiom 기다려, 멈춰; 견뎌 내다
If you ask someone to hold on, you are asking them to wait for a short time.

복습 **weird** [wiərd] a. 기이한, 기묘한; 기괴한, 섬뜩한
If you describe something or someone as weird, you mean that they are strange.

beat it idiom 떠나다; 저리 가!
If you beat it, you leave immediately.

복습 **mess up** idiom 실수하다; ~을 엉망으로 만들다; 혼란스럽게 하다
If you mess something up, you do something badly or incorrectly.

‡ **familiar** [fəmíljər] a. 친숙한, 잘 알고 있는; 친한; 잘 알려진
If someone or something is familiar to you, you recognize them or know them well.

‡ **fancy** [fǽnsi] a. 장식이 많은; 고급의; 복잡한; v. 생각하다, 상상하다
If you describe something as fancy, you mean that it is special, unusual, or elaborate, for example because it has a lot of decoration.

canopy [kǽnəpi] n. (가게·건물 등의) 차양; (늘어뜨린) 덮개
A capony is a curved covering over part of a building.

‡ **neighbor** [néibər] n. 이웃; 동료; 동포 (neighborhood n. 인근, 근처)
A neighborhood is one of the parts of a town where people live.

doorman [dɔ́:rmæn] n. (호텔·극장 등의) 수위, 문지기
A doorman is a person whose job is to stay by the main entrance of a large building, and help people visiting the building.

* **fake** [feik] a. 가짜의, 거짓된; 모조의; n. 모조품; v. ~인 척하다
A fake fur or a fake painting, for example, is a fur or painting that has been made to look valuable or genuine, often in order to deceive people.

* **bush** [buʃ] n. 관목, 덤불; 우거진 것
A bush is a large plant which is smaller than a tree and has a lot of branches.

* **tag** [tæg] n. 꼬리표; v. 꼬리표를 붙이다
A tag is a small piece of card or cloth which is attached to an object or person and has information about that object or person on it.

* **realistic** [ri:əlístik] a. 사실적인, 실제 그대로의; 현실적인; 실현 가능한
You say that a painting, story, or film is realistic when the people and things in it are like people and things in real life.

* **last** [læst] v. 오래가다; (특정한 시간 동안) 계속되다; 견디다; ad. 맨 끝에, 마지막에
If something lasts for a particular length of time, it continues to be able to be used for that time, for example because there is some of it left or because it is in good enough condition.

gulp [gʌlp] v. 침을 꿀떡 삼키다; (숨을) 깊이 들이마시다; n. 꿀꺽 마시기
If you gulp, you swallow air, often making a noise in your throat as you do so, because you are nervous or excited.

* **awful** [ɔ́:fəl] a. 끔찍한, 지독한; (정도가) 대단한, 아주 심한
If you say that something is awful, you mean that it is extremely unpleasant, shocking, or bad.

no matter how idiom 아무리 ~해도
You use no matter in expressions such as 'no matter how' and 'no matter what' to say that something is true or happens in all circumstances.

puke [pju:k] v. 토하다
When someone pukes, they empty the contents of the stomach through the mouth.

manhole [mǽnhòul] n. (도로 등의) 맨홀
A manhole is a large hole in a road or path, covered by a metal plate that can be removed.

barricade [bǽrəkèid] n. 바리케이드, 장애물; v. 방어벽을 치다
A barricade is a line of vehicles or other objects placed across a road or open space to stop people getting past, for example during street fighting or as a protest.

ᵃ sign [sain] n. 표지판; 몸짓, 신호; 기색, 흔적; v. 서명하다; 신호를 보내다
A sign is a piece of wood, metal, or plastic with words or pictures on it. Signs give you information about something, or give you a warning or an instruction.

ᵃ opening [óupəniŋ] n. 구멍, 틈; 시작 부분; 개막식; 공석
An opening is a hole or empty space through which things or people can pass.

ᵃ painful [péinfəl] a. (몸이) 아픈; (마음이) 괴로운, 고통스러운; 골치아픈
If a part of your body is painful, it hurts because it is injured or because there is something wrong with it.

ᵃ mention [ménʃən] v. 말하다, 언급하다; n. 언급, 거론
If you mention something, you say something about it, usually briefly.

ᵃ illegal [ilíːgəl] a. 불법적인
If something is illegal, the law says that it is not allowed.

sewer [suːər] n. 하수관, 수채통
A sewer is a large underground channel that carries waste matter and rain water away, usually to a place where it is treated and made harmless.

ᵃ gross [grous] a. 역겨운; 아주 무례한; ad. 모두 (합해서)
If you describe something as gross, you think it is very unpleasant.

ᵃ race [reis] v. 쏜살같이 가다; 경주하다; n. 경주; 인종
If you race somewhere, you go there as quickly as possible.

stoop [stuːp] v. 몸을 굽히다; n. 구부정한 자세
If you stoop, you bend your body forward and downward.

scary [skέəri] a. 무서운, 겁나는
Something that is scary is rather frightening.

holster [hóulstər] n. (벨트에 차는 가죽) 권총집
A holster is a holder for a small gun, which is worn on a belt around someone's waist or on a strap around their shoulder.

soak [souk] v. 흠뻑 적시다; 스며들다; n. 목욕; (액체 속에) 담그기
If a liquid soaks something or if you soak something with a liquid, the liquid makes the thing very wet.

officer [ɔ́ːfisər] n. 경찰관; 장교; 직원
Members of the police force can be referred to as officers.

temporary [témpərèri] a. 일시적인, 임시의 (temporarily ad. 일시적으로)
Something that is temporary lasts for only a limited time.

slip [slip] v. 슬며시 가다; 미끄러지다; n. (작은 종이) 조각; 미끄러짐
(slip one's mind idiom 깜빡 잊어 버리다)
If something slips your mind, you forget about it.

all over the place idiom 두서없는; 엉망인; 모든 곳에, 사방에
If you say that someone is all over the place, you mean that they are confused or disorganized, and unable to think clearly or act properly.

take off idiom (서둘러) 떠나다; 날아오르다
If you take off or take yourself off, you go away, often suddenly and unexpectedly.

get rid of idiom ~을 처리하다, 없애다
If you get rid of someone who is causing problems for you or who you do not like, you do something to prevent them affecting you any more, for example by making them leave.

newsstand [njúːzstænd] n. (신문·잡지) 판매점, 가판대
A newsstand is a stall in the street or a public place, which sells newspapers and magazines.

front page [frʌnt péidʒ] n. (신문의) 제1면
A front-page article or picture appears on the front page of a newspaper because it is very important or interesting.

⁎ **headline** [hédlain] n. (신문 기사의) 표제; v. (기사에) 표제를 달다
A headline is the title of a newspaper story, printed in large letters at the top of the story, especially on the front page.

⁎ **citizen** [sítəzən] n. 시민; 주민
The citizens of a town or city are the people who live there.

⁑ **warn** [wɔːrn] v. 경고하다, 주의를 주다
If you warn someone not to do something, you advise them not to do it so that they can avoid possible danger or punishment.

take a chance idiom (위험한) 모험을 시도하다, 운에 맡기고 한 번 해 보다
When you take a chance, you try to do something although there is a large risk of danger or failure.

복습 **peek** [piːk] v. (재빨리) 훔쳐보다; 살짝 보이다; n. 엿보기
If you peek at something or someone, you have a quick look at them, often secretly.

⁑ **observe** [əbzɔ́ːrv] v. 관찰하다; ~을 보다; (발언·논평·의견을) 말하다
If you observe a person or thing, you watch them carefully, especially in order to learn something about them.

⁑ **attempt** [ətémpt] v. 시도하다, 애써 해 보다; n. 시도
If you attempt to do something, especially something difficult, you try to do it.

⁎ **alternate** [ɔ́ːltərnèit] a. 대체의, 대신의; 교대의; v. 번갈아 나오게 하다
You use alternate to describe a plan, idea, or system which is different from the one already in operation and can be used instead of it.

institute [ínstətjùːt] n. 기관, 협회; v. 도입하다; (절차를) 시작하다

An institute is an organization set up to do a particular type of work, especially research or teaching.

vicinity [visínəti] n. (~의) 부근, 인근 (in the vicinity of idiom 대략)

You use in the vicinity of before a number to show that it is not exact.

approximate [əpráksəmət] a. 대략의, 근접한; v. 가까워지다
(approximately ad. 거의)

An approximate number, time, or position is close to the correct number, time, or position, but is not exact.

rumor [rúːmər] v. 소문이 있다; n. 소문, 유언비어

If something is rumored to be the case, people are suggesting that it is the case, but they do not know for certain.

yikes [jaiks] int. 이크, 으악 (놀랐을 때 내는 소리)

Yikes is used to show that you are worried, surprised, or shocked.

slam [slæm] v. 쾅 닫다; 세게 치다, 놓다; n. 쾅 하고 닫기; 탕 하는 소리

If you slam a door or window or if it slams, it shuts noisily and with great force.

Chapter
6

1. Why did Zack tell Zeke's dad the truth?

   A. He did not have another option.

   B. He was tired of lying.

   C. He felt bad for Zeke's dad.

   D. He trusted Zeke's dad like his own dad.

2. What really surprised Zeke's dad?

   A. That Zack looked like his son

   B. That Zack did not like Newer York

   C. That Zeke lost his retainer

   D. That Zeke ran away from home

3. Why did Zeke's dad believe everything Zack said?

   A. He had been to Zack's universe many times before.

   B. He knew many people from other universes.

   C. It was common knowledge that Zack's universe existed.

   D. There were a lot of famous books on parallel universes.

4. What was NOT true?

   A. Opening Day was almost over.

   B. Opening Day would end at midnight.

   C. Zeke's dad knew how to help Zack.

   D. Zeke's dad would not go to Zack's universe.

5. What did Zeke's dad tell Zack to do?

   A. Close his eyes and think about something else

   B. Stare at the medicine cabinet until it moved

   C. Remove his hand from the medicine cabinet door

   D. Imagine the back of the medicine cabinet opening

Check Your Reading Speed
1분에 몇 단어를 읽는지 리딩 속도를 측정해보세요.

$$\frac{584 \ words}{reading \ time \ (\quad) \ sec} \times 60 = (\quad) \ WPM$$

Build Your Vocabulary

out of breath idiom 숨이 가쁜
If you are out of breath, you are breathing very quickly and with difficulty because you have been doing something energetic.

hallway [hɔ́:lwèi] n. 현관; 통로; 복도
A hallway in a house or apartment is the area just inside the front door, into which some of the other rooms open.

복습 **race** [reis] v. 쏜살같이 가다; 경주하다; n. 경주; 인종
If you race somewhere, you go there as quickly as possible.

복습 **medicine** [médəsin] n. 약, 약물; 의학, 의술; 의료
Medicine is a substance that you drink or swallow in order to cure an illness.

복습 **cabinet** [kǽbənit] n. 캐비닛, 보관장; (정부의) 내각
A cabinet is a cupboard used for storing things such as medicine or alcoholic drinks or for displaying decorative things in.

복습 **budge** [bʌdʒ] v. 약간 움직이다, 꼼짝하다; 의견을 바꾸다
If someone or something will not budge, they will not move. If you cannot budge them, you cannot make them move.

‡ **obvious** [ábviəs] a. 분명한, 확실한; 명백한 (obviously ad. 분명히)
You use obviously to indicate that something is easily noticed, seen, or recognized.

^복_습 **universe** [júːnəvəːrs] n. 우주; 은하계; (특정한 유형의) 경험 세계
A universe can be a world or an area of space that is different from the one we are in.

* **whirl** [hwəːrl] v. 빙그르르 돌다; (마음·생각 등이) 혼란스럽다; n. 빙빙 돌기
If something or someone whirls around or if you whirl them around, they move around or turn around very quickly.

‡ **enemy** [énəmi] n. 적; 적군; 장애물
If someone is your enemy, they hate you or want to harm you.

run out idiom (시간·돈 등이) 없어지다, 다 되다
If time is running out, you do not have long to do something.

* **incredible** [inkrédəbl] a. 믿을 수 없는, 믿기 힘든
If you say that something is incredible, you mean that it is very unusual or surprising, and you cannot believe it is really true, although it may be.

^복_습 **parallel** [pǽrəlèl] a. 아주 유사한; 평행한; n. ~와 아주 유사한 것; v. ~와 유사하다
Parallel events or situations happen at the same time as one another, or are similar to one another.

^복_습 **camp** [kæmp] n. (합숙) 캠프; 야영지, 텐트; v. 야영하다 (training camp n. 훈련 캠프)
A training camp for soldiers or sports players is an organized period of training at a particular place.

^복_습 **retainer** [ritéinər] n. 치아 교정 장치
A retainer is a device that you wear in your mouth helps to straighten your teeth.

* **smack** [smæk] v. 탁 소리가 나게 치다; 세게 부딪치다; n. 강타; ad. 정통으로
If you smack someone, you hit them with your hand.

* **forehead** [fɔ́ːrhèd] n. 이마
Your forehead is the area at the front of your head between your eyebrows and your hair.

‡ swear [swɛər] v. 맹세하다; 욕을 하다
If you say that you swear that something is true or that you can swear to it, you are saying very firmly that it is true.

daze [deiz] v. 멍하게 하다; 눈부시게 하다; n. 멍한 상태; 눈이 부심 (dazed a. 멍한)
If someone is dazed, they are confused and unable to think clearly, often because of shock or a blow to the head.

‡ stuff [stʌf] n. 일, 것, 물건; v. 박제하다; 쑤셔 넣다; 채워 넣다
You can use stuff to refer to things such as a substance, a collection of things, events, or ideas, or the contents of something in a general way without mentioning the thing itself by name.

blah [blɑ:] int. 어쩌고저쩌고
You use 'blah, blah, blah' to refer to something that is said or written without giving the actual words, because you think that they are boring or unimportant.

touchy [tʌ́ʃi] a. (주제가) 민감한; (사람이) 화를 잘 내는, 과민한
If you say that something is a touchy subject, you mean that it is a subject that needs to be dealt with carefully and in a sensitive way, because it might upset or offend people.

‡ subject [sʌ́bdʒikt] n. (논의 등의) 주제; 과목; 연구 대상; a. ~에 달려 있는; v. 종속시키다
The subject of something such as a conversation, letter, or book is the thing that is being discussed or written about.

‡ slip [slip] v. 슬며시 가다; 미끄러지다; n. (작은 종이) 조각; 미끄러짐
If you slip somewhere, you go there quickly and quietly.

‡ nod [nad] v. (고개를) 끄덕이다, 까딱하다; n. (고개를) 끄덕임
If you nod, you move your head downward and upward to show that you are answering 'yes' to a question, or to show agreement, understanding, or approval.

‡ attention [əténʃən] n. 주의, 주목; 관심
If you give someone or something your attention, you look at it, listen to it, or think about it carefully.

‡ complete [kəmplíːt] a. 완전한; 완벽한; v. 완료하다, 끝마치다 (completely ad. 완전히)
You can use complete to emphasize that you are referring to the whole of something and not just part of it.

복습 exact [igzǽkt] a. 정확한; 꼼꼼한, 빈틈없는 (exactly ad. 정확히)
You use exactly before an amount, number, or position to emphasize that it is no more, no less, or no different from what you are stating.

＊miserable [mízərəbl] a. 비참한; 우울하게 하는; 보잘것없는
If you are miserable, you are very unhappy.

visualize [víʒuəlàiz] v. 마음속에 그려 보다, 상상하다
If you visualize something, you imagine what it is like by forming a mental picture of it.

springy [spríŋi] a. 용수철 같은, 탄성이 있는; 생기 넘치는
If something is springy, it returns quickly to its original shape after you press it.

in time idiom (~에) 시간 맞춰, 늦지 않게
If you are in time for a particular event or to do something, you are not too late for it.

복습 melt [melt] v. 녹다; (감정 등이) 누그러지다; n. 용해
When a solid substance melts or when you melt it, it changes to a liquid, usually because it has been heated.

Chapter 7

1. **Why was Zeke already planning to return home?**

   A. He knew his dad was worried.

   B. He preferred being in his universe.

   C. He wanted to check that Zack was all right.

   D. He was being forced to leave by Zack's dad.

2. **What did Zack's dad and Zeke's dad do when they saw each other?**

   A. They introduced themselves for the first time.

   B. They blamed each other for mixing up their kids.

   C. They greeted each other like friends.

   D. They hesitated to speak to each other.

3. How did Zack's dad and Zeke dad's meet?

   A. Through a medicine cabinet

   B. Through a laundry basket

   C. Through a sock drawer

   D. Through a clothes dryer

4. Where was Zack's retainer and why was it there?

   A. It was in Zeke's pocket because Zeke had taken it.

   B. It was with Zack's dad because his dad had found it.

   C. It was on the bathroom floor because Zack had dropped it there.

   D. It was in the medicine cabinet because Zack had left it there.

5. What happened after Zack and Zeke said good-bye?

   A. They still visited each other once in a while.

   B. Zack sometimes thought about Zeke.

   C. Zeke sent secret messages to Zack.

   D. Zack assumed he would never see Zeke again.

Check Your Reading Speed
1분에 몇 단어를 읽는지 리딩 속도를 측정해보세요.

$$\frac{528 \; words}{reading \; time \; (\quad) \; sec} \times 60 = (\qquad) \; WPM$$

Build Your Vocabulary

familiar [fəmíljər] a. 친숙한, 잘 알고 있는; 친한; 잘 알려진
If someone or something is familiar to you, you recognize them or know them well.

thank heavens idiom 정말 다행이다
You say 'Thank God' or 'Thank heavens' when you are very relieved about something.

embarrass [imbǽrəs] v. 당황스럽게 하다; 곤란하게 하다 (embarrassed a. 당황스러운)
A person who is embarrassed feels shy, ashamed, or guilty about something.

homesick [hóumsìk] a. 향수병을 앓는, 향수에 잠긴
If you are homesick, you feel unhappy because you are away from home and are missing your family, friends, and home very much.

awful [ɔ́:fəl] a. (정도가) 대단한, 아주 심한; 끔찍한, 지독한 (awfully ad. 정말, 몹시)
You use awfully to emphasize what you are saying.

universe [jú:nəvə:rs] n. 우주; 은하계; (특정한 유형의) 경험 세계
A universe can be a world or an area of space that is different from the one we are in.

figure [fígjər] v. 생각하다; 중요하다; n. (멀리서 흐릿하게 보이는) 사람; 수치
If you figure that something is the case, you think or guess that it is the case.

^복_습**medicine** [médəsin] n. 약, 약물; 의학, 의술, 의료
Medicine is a substance that you drink or swallow in order to cure an illness.

^복_습**cabinet** [kǽbənit] n. 캐비닛, 보관장; (정부의) 내각
A cabinet is a cupboard used for storing things such as medicine or alcoholic drinks or for displaying decorative things in.

* **amaze** [əméiz] v. (대단히) 놀라게 하다; 경악하게 하다 (amazed a. 놀란)
If something amazes you, it surprises you very much.

laundromat [lɔ́:ndrəmæt] n. (동전을 넣고 사용하는) 빨래방
A laundromat is a place where people can pay to use machines to wash and dry their clothes.

^복_습**odd** [ad] a. (신발·양말·장갑 등이) 한 짝만 있는; 홀수의; 이상한, 특이한
You say that two things are odd when they do not belong to the same set or pair.

^복_습**laundry** [lɔ́:ndri] n. 세탁; 세탁물
Laundry is used to refer to clothes, sheets, and towels that are about to be washed, are being washed, or have just been washed.

^복_습**parallel** [pǽrəlèl] a. 아주 유사한; 평행한; n. ~와 아주 유사한 것; v. ~와 유사하다
Parallel events or situations happen at the same time as one another, or are similar to one another.

^복_습**opening** [óupəniŋ] n. 구멍, 틈; 시작 부분; 개막식; 공석
An opening is a hole or empty space through which things or people can pass.

laugh one's head off idiom 자지러지게 웃다, 몹시 웃어대다
If you say that someone laughs their head off, you emphasize that they are laughing a lot or very loudly.

* **interrupt** [intərʌ́pt] v. (말·행동을) 방해하다; 중단시키다; 차단하다
If you interrupt someone who is speaking, you say or do something that causes them to stop.

^복_습 **camp** [kæmp] n. (합숙) 캠프; 야영지, 텐트; v. 야영하다 (training camp n. 훈련 캠프)
A training camp for soldiers or sports players is an organized period of training at a particular place.

^복_습 **crawl** [krɔːl] v. 기어가다; 우글거리다; n. 기어가기
When you crawl, you move forward on your hands and knees.

＊**jerk** [dʒəːrk] n. 얼간이; 홱 움직임; v. 홱 움직이다
If you call someone a jerk, you are insulting them because you think they are stupid or you do not like them.

^복_습 **cab** [kæb] n. 택시
A cab is a taxi.

＊**horn** [hɔːrn] n. (차량의) 경적; (양·소 등의) 뿔; 나팔
On a vehicle such as a car, the horn is the device that makes a loud noise as a signal or warning.

honk [haŋk] v. (자동차 경적을) 울리다; n. 빵빵 (자동차 경적 소리)
If you honk the horn of a vehicle or if the horn honks, you make the horn produce a short loud sound.

so long int. 안녕 (작별 인사)
You can use so long as an informal way of saying goodbye.

fish out idiom ~을 꺼내다
If you fish something out from somewhere, you take or pull it out, often after searching for it for some time.

^복_습 **retainer** [ritéinər] n. 치아 교정 장치
A retainer is a device that you wear in your mouth helps to straighten your teeth.

swipe [swaip] v. ~을 훔치다; 후려치다; n. 후려치기, 휘두르기
If you swipe something, you take it away quickly without permission of the owner.

복습 nod [nad] v. (고개를) 끄덕이다, 까딱하다; n. (고개를) 끄덕임
If you nod, you move your head downward and upward to show that you are answering 'yes' to a question, or to show agreement, understanding, or approval.

sheepish [ʃíːpiʃ] a. 당황해하는 (sheepishly ad. 겸연쩍게, 멋쩍게)
If you look sheepish, you look slightly embarrassed because you feel foolish or you have done something silly.

fit [fit] v. (모양·크기가) 맞다; 어울리게 하다; 적절하다; a. 건강한; 적합한, 알맞은
If something fits, it is the right size and shape to go onto a person's body or onto a particular object.

복습 hallway [hɔ́ːlwèi] n. 현관; 통로; 복도
A hallway in a house or apartment is the area just inside the front door, into which some of the other rooms open.

★ chime [ʧaim] v. (종이나 시계가) 울리다; (노래하듯) 말하다; n. 차임, 종
When a bell or a clock chimes, it makes ringing sounds.

복습 wave [weiv] v. (손·팔을) 흔들다; 손짓하다; n. 파도, 물결; 흔들기
If you wave or wave your hand, you move your hand from side to side in the air, usually in order to say hello or goodbye to someone.

face [feis] v. 마주보다; 직면하다; n. 얼굴; 표정
If someone or something faces a particular thing, person, or direction, they are positioned opposite them or are looking in that direction.

★ shelf [ʃelf] n. (pl. shelves) 선반; (책장의) 칸
A shelf is a flat piece of wood, metal, or glass which is attached to a wall or to the sides of a cupboard.

복습 visualize [víʒuəlàiz] v. 마음속에 그려 보다, 상상하다
If you visualize something, you imagine what it is like by forming a mental picture of it.

discover [diskʌ́vər] v. 찾다, 알아내다; 발견하다; 발굴하다
If you discover something that you did not know about before, you become aware of it or learn of it.

^{복습} **weird** [wiərd] a. 기이한, 기묘한; 기괴한, 섬뜩한

If you describe something or someone as weird, you mean that they are strange.

^{복습} **except** [iksépt] prep. (~을) 제외하고는

You use except to introduce the only thing or person that a statement does not apply to, or a fact that prevents a statement from being completely true.

번역

1장

저는 지극히 평범하다고 사람들이 생각할 아이입니다. 제 이름은 잭(Zack)이며, 그것은 정말 특별할 것 없는 이름입니다. 저는 열 살인데, 꽤 평범한 나이이죠. 제 머리카락과 눈은 평범한 갈색입니다. 저는 치아가 살짝 삐뚤어졌는데, 그것도 제 나이 때는 다 그렇습니다. 그리고 저는 뉴욕(New York)에 있는 큰 아파트 건물에 삽니다. 적어도 제가 여러분에게 말하려는 그 일이 일어나기 전까지는, 제가 사는 건물이 평범하다고 저는 항상 생각했습니다.

제가 기이한 일들에 항상 관심이 있었다는 것을 인정합니다. 밤에 무덤 밖으로 기어 나오는 죽은 사람들 같은 일 말이에요. 아니면 여러분을 지켜보다가 갑자기 머리가 폭발해 버리는 사람들 같은 것들이요. 저는 그런 일들을 실제로 본 적은 없습니다. 하지만 그런 일들이 일어날 리 없다고 제가 감히 말할 수 있을까요?

어쨌든, 제가 여러분에게 말하고 싶은 순간은 봄방학이 시작될 때 일어났습니다. 아빠는 저를 플로리다주(Florida)에 데리고 가려고 준비를 했습니다. 우리는 뉴욕 양키스(New York Yankees) 팀의 봄 훈련 캠프에 갈 예정이었습니다.

제 부모님은 이혼했습니다. 저는 일부 기간 동안 아빠와 삽니다. 아빠는 작가이고, 멋진 일들을 많이 할 수 있습니다. 봄 훈련에 가서 그것에 대해 잡지에 기사를 쓰는 일 같은 것을 하지요. 이런 일을 하고 아빠가 돈을 받는다는 것을 저는 믿을 수 없습니다. 아빠도 마찬가지랍니다.

우리가 떠나기로 계획한 날은 토요일 아침이었습니다. 저는 정말 신이 나서, 새벽 여섯 시쯤 잠에서 깼습니다. 눈을 뜨자마자, 저는 뭔가 깨달았습니다. 잠자기 전에 제 입 안에 치아 교정 유지 장치를 끼우는 것을 잊어버렸던 것입니다. 그건 도대체 어디에 있을까요?

치아 교정 유지 장치는, 여러분이 모를 수도 있으니 설명하자면, 밤에 치아에 끼우는 교정기입니다. 저는 제 유지 장치를 전혀 좋아하지 않습니다. 그것은 철사와 분홍색 플라스틱으로 만들어졌습니다. 그것은 정말 역겹게 생겼는데, 특히 점심시간에 당신이 그것을 빼서 식탁 위에 올려놓을 때 그렇습니다.

아빠는 제가 유지 장치를 잃어버리는 것을 싫어합니다. 제 생각에, 그것은 1,200달러입니다. 아니면 112달러입니다. 어느 쪽이었는지는 잊어버렸습니다.

저는 유지 장치 하나를 청바지 안에 두었는데, 그게 세탁되고 말았습니다. 그것은 주머니 안에서 녹아 버렸습니다.

62 THROUGH THE MEDICINE CABINET

하나는 레아 할머니(Grandma Leah)의 음식물 쓰레기 분쇄기 안에서 엉망으로 부숴졌습니다. 다른 하나는 변기 안으로 쓸려 내려가 버렸습니다. 또 다른 것은 제가 방에 없는 동안 도둑이 훔쳐갔다고 저는 거의 확신합니다. 비록 제가 그 사실을 입증할 수 없었지만 말입니다.

전부 다 해서, 저는 그것을 일곱 개 이상 잃어버린 적은 없습니다. 많아도, 여덟 개일 것입니다.

저는 제 유지 장치가 원래 있었어야 할, 제 입 안이 아니라, 욕실에 있는 약장에 있다고 확신했습니다. 저는 자리에서 일어나서 약장 문을 열었습니다. 그렇지! 제 유지 장치는 거기 있었습니다. 그러나 그때, 제가 약장 문을 막 닫으려고 할 때, 기이한 일이 일어났습니다. 정말 기이한 일이요. 약장의 뒷부분이 열렸습니다. 그리고 거기에는, 제 얼굴을 똑바로 쳐다보고 있는, 저와 거의 똑같이 생긴 한 소년이 있었습니다!

2장

나와 똑같이 생긴 남자아이라고? 그게 어떻게 가능하지? 저는 너무나 놀라서, 제 유지 장치를 쳤습니다. 그것은 그 아이의 욕실로 떨어졌습니다. 그때 우리

둘 다 소리를 질렀고 우리의 약장 문을 쾅 닫았습니다.

도대체 여기에서 무슨 일이 일어나고 있는 걸까요?

저는 약장을 아주 천천히 다시 열었습니다. 아니요. 반대편에는 아무도 없었습니다. 저는 약장의 뒷부분을 밀었습니다. 그것은 열리지 않았습니다. 정말 기이했습니다.

그렇다면 제 유지 장치는 어디에 있을까요? 저는 옆집의 아파트를 확인해 보는 게 좋겠다고 생각했습니다. 타라다시 부인(Mrs. Taradash)이라는 이름의 나이 많은 여자가 거기 살고 있습니다.

타라다시 부인은 좀 까다로운 사람입니다. 제가 제 방 벽에 설치한 농구 골대를 그녀가 그다지 마음에 들어 하지 않는다는 것을 저는 알고 있습니다. 그녀는 아빠에게 여러 번 항의했습니다. 제가 슬램 덩크(slam-dunk)를 하면, 그것이 마치 리히터 척도(Richter Scale) 진도 5.7 같다고 그녀는 말합니다.

그런데 아마 타라다시 부인에게 손자가 있을 겁니다. 어쩌면 부인의 손자가 저와 거의 똑같이 생겼을지도 모릅니다. 그리고 아마도 그녀의 약장이 우리 약장 반대편 벽에 걸려 있을지도 모릅니다.

이 설명이 정말 말이 안 된다는 것을 저는 알고 있습니다. 하지만 그건 제가

생각해낼 수 있는 전부입니다.

저는 옷을 입었습니다. 그다음에 저는 우리 아파트 밖으로 조용히 살짝 빠져나왔습니다. 저는 타라다시 부인 집의 문을 두드렸습니다. 아무 대답이 없었습니다. 저는 다시 두드렸습니다. 누군가 문을 열기까지 시간이 좀 걸렸습니다. 타라다시 부인은 털이 북슬북슬한 가운을 입고 북슬북슬한 슬리퍼를 신고 있었습니다. 그녀의 머리카락은 온통 헝클어져 있었습니다. 그리고 그녀는 자신의 두 눈을 비비고 있었습니다. 사실을 알고 싶다면, 부인은 저를 보고 기분이 썩 좋아 보이지 않았습니다.

"귀찮게 해서 죄송합니다. 타라다시 아주머니." 저는 말했습니다. "제 유지 장치를 아주머니의 욕실에서 꺼낼 수 있을까 해서요."

"너의 무엇을 말하는 거니, 귀염둥이야?" 그녀가 말했습니다.

그녀는 모든 아이들을 "귀염둥이"라고 부릅니다. 하지만 실제로 그녀가 그렇게 생각하지 않는다는 것을 여러분도 알 수 있지요.

"제 치아 유지 장치요." 제가 대답했습니다.

"그게 도대체 뭐니, 귀염둥이야?"

"치아 유지 장치는 철사와 분홍색 플라스틱으로 만든 교정기인데, 그건 가끔 음식물 쓰레기 처리나 변기에 떨어지기도 해요." 제가 설명했습니다. "아주머니의 손자가 약장 문을 열었을 때 제 유지 장치가 아주머니의 아파트 안으로 떨어졌어요."

타라다시 부인은 제가 정신 나간 사람이라도 한 것처럼 저를 바라보았습니다.

"내게 손자가 없단다, 귀염둥이야." 그녀가 말했습니다.

"손자가 없다고요? 그렇다면 방금 제 약장의 반대편을 연 사람은 누구예요?"

그녀의 얼굴 절반의 아래쪽은 미소를 지었습니다. 그러나 위쪽 절반은 인상을 쓰고 있었습니다. 반으로 나뉜 두 부분이 서로 싸우고 있는 것 같았습니다. 그녀는 제 발 위로 문을 닫으려고 했습니다.

"제발 문을 닫지 마세요, 타라다시 아주머니." 저는 부인에게 간청했습니다. "저는 제 유지 장치를 아주머니의 아파트에서 잃어버렸어요. 제가 잃어버린 여덟 번째 장치예요. 어쩌면 아홉 번째일지도 몰라요. 제가 그것을 되찾지 못한다면, 아빠한테 엄청 혼날 거예요. 아주머니도 그런 일이 양심에 걸리길 바라지 않잖아요, 그렇죠?"

그녀가 문을 열었고 저를 바라보았습니다.

"네가 원하는 게 뭐니?" 그녀가 말했습니다. 말을 한다기보다 낮게 쉭쉭거리는 소리에 더 가까웠습니다. 그리고 그녀는 "귀염둥이"라고 말하는 것을 잊어버린 것 같았습니다.

"제 유지 장치만 찾으면 돼요." 저는 말했습니다. "그게 제 약장에서 아주머니의 욕실로 떨어졌다는 걸 아주머니의 손자가 아닌 그 남자아이가 말해 줄 거예요. 제발 그저 제가 그것을 좀 찾아볼 수 있게 해 주세요."

"네가 찾아보도록 내가 허락해 주면." 그녀가 말했습니다. "너는 내가 다시 잘 수 있게 떠날 거니?"

"그럼요, 아주머니." 제가 말했습니다.

그녀가 깊은 한숨을 쉬었습니다. 그러고 나서 그녀는 저에게 아파트 안으로 들어오라고 손짓했습니다.

저는 안으로 들어갔습니다.

이상했습니다. 보이는 모든 곳에, 솜으로 속을 채운 동물들이 있었습니다. 그리고 저는 껴안을 수 있는 곰 인형을 말하는 것도 아닙니다. 무슨 말인가 하면 박제사가 속을 채워 넣은 진짜로 죽은 동물들이 있다는 거예요. 청설모, 토끼, 비버, 얼룩 다람쥐 같은 것들이요. 그것들은 모두 기이한 자세로 굳어 있었습니다. 그리고 그것들은 반짝거리는 유리 눈으로 사람들을 지켜보고 있었습니다. 그것들은 정말 저를 소름 끼치게 했습니다.

저는 서둘러 욕실 안으로 들어가서 둘러보았습니다. 욕실 바닥에도 다른 어느 곳에도 유지 장치가 없었습니다. 저는 약장을 열었습니다. 저는 약장 뒷부분을 밀어 보았습니다. 그것은 꼼짝도 하지 않았습니다. 그래서 저는 약장 문을 닫았습니다.

"만족하니?" 그녀가 낮게 쉭쉭거리듯 말했습니다.

제가 떠나지 않으면 그녀의 두 눈이 벌겋게 빛을 내기 시작할 거라는 느낌이 갑자기 들었습니다. 그리고 나서 그녀는 저를 붙잡아서 제 속을 채워 넣으려고 하겠지요. 저도 그곳에서, 이상하게 굳은 자세로 다른 동물들 옆에 나란히 서서, 반짝거리는 유리 눈으로 손님들을 바라보고 있겠지요.

저는 사과했고 아빠의 아파트로 서둘러 돌아왔습니다. 무슨 일이 일어났는지 저는 전혀 알 수 없었습니다. 제가 그 모든 것들에 대해 꿈꾼 거라고 저는 생각하기 시작했습니다. 그런데 제가 만약 꿈을 꾼 거라면, 제 유지 장치는 어디에 있을까요?

제 침실로 돌아오는 길에, 저는 제 욕실을 지나쳤습니다. 곁눈질로 저는 무언가를 본 것 같았습니다.

제 약장 문이 있잖아요.

그것이 천천히 슬금슬금 열리고 있었어요.

번역

3장

저는 제 욕실로 달려갔습니다. 저는 약장 문을 확 잡아당겨 완전히 열었습니다.

거기에 그 아이가 있었습니다! 제가 전에 봤던 것과 똑같은 소년이었습니다.

"야!" 제가 말했습니다.

그는 이번에는 문을 쾅 닫지 않았습니다. 제가 생각하기에 그는 몹시 놀란 것 같았습니다. 그는 계속 빤히 쳐다보고 있었습니다. 저 또한 빤히 쳐다보고 있었습니다. 그는 정말로 저와 아주 많이 닮아 보였습니다. 단지 그의 치아가 저보다 훨씬 더 많이 삐뚤어져 있었습니다.

"넌 누구야?" 제가 물었습니다.

"제크(Zeke)야." 그가 말했습니다.

"나는 잭이야."

"알아."

"너 옆집에 사는 거 아니지." 제가 말했습니다. "맞지?"

그는 고개를 가로저었습니다.

"그러면 넌 어디에 살아?"

"다른 어떤 곳이야. 가까이에 있는 어떤 곳이지만, 좀 멀리 떨어진 곳. 어쩌면 네가 이상하다고 생각할지도 모르는 곳이지."

"너 뉴저지주(New Jersey)에 사니?"

그는 고개를 가로저었습니다.

"그럼 어디?"

"뉴어욕(Newer York)이라고 들어 본 적 있어?" 그가 말했습니다.

"포킵시(Poughkeepsie) 근처의 북쪽에 있는 거야?" 제가 물었습니다.

그는 한숨을 쉬었고 제가 세상에서 가장 멍청한 소리를 한 것처럼 눈을 굴렸습니다. 저는 갑자기 어떤 생각이 났습니다.

"있지." 제가 말했습니다. "이거 혹시 내가 끼어들었다가 후회하게 될 그런 괴상한 일이야?"

"나는 질문 하나만 더 대답할 시간이 있어." 그가 말했습니다. "그러고 나서 나는 가 봐야 해."

"알겠어." 제가 말했습니다. "내 유지 장치를 네가 가지고 있어? 그게 네 쪽으로 떨어진 것 같아."

그는 갑자기 문을 닫으려고 했습니다. 그러나 저는 그 애가 상대하기에 너무 빨랐습니다. 저는 제 팔을 약장 안으로 찔러 넣었습니다. 그 바람에 그는 문을 닫지 못했습니다. 그는 제 손을 붙잡았고 약장 문에서 떼어 내려고 했습니다. 저는 그의 손목을 잡았습니다.

"이거 놔!" 그가 외쳤습니다.

"내 유지 장치를 주기 전까진 안 돼!"

그는 벗어나려고 했습니다. 저는 단단히 붙잡았습니다. 그는 뒤로 물러났습니다. 저는 양손으로 매달렸습니다.

그는 약장 사이로 저를 잡아당겼습니다. 그러자 우리 둘 다 그의 욕실 안의 바닥으로 떨어졌습니다.

"이제 네가 저질러 버렸어!" 그가 외쳤습니다. "이제 네가 진짜로 저질러 버렸다고!" 그는 겁을 먹은 것 같았습니다.

"뭘 저질렀는데?" 제가 물었습니다.

"그 누구도 하면 안 되는 바로 그 일 말이야." 그가 말했습니다.

"그게 뭔데?" 제가 물었습니다.

"평행 우주로 건너가는 일 말이야!"

4장

"평행 우주가 도대체 뭐야?" 제가 물었습니다.

제크는 초조하게 주변을 둘러보았습니다.

"쉬이이잇!" 그가 외쳤습니다. "누가 네 말을 들을지도 몰라!"

"크게 소리지르는 사람은 바로 너야." 제가 말했습니다. "도대체 평행 우주가 뭔데?"

"음, 그건 이런 거야." 제크가 말했습니다. "우리 우주는 너희의 우주 바로 옆에 있어. 너무 가까이 있어서 네가 믿지 못할 정도이지. 심지어 그것은 너희의 우주와 같은 공간의 일부를 차지하고 있어. 대부분의 경우 너희는 우리를 볼 수 없을 뿐이지. 구멍이 열리는 날(Opening Day)을 제외하고 말이야. 오늘처럼."

"오늘은 개막식 날(Opening Day)이 아니야." 제가 말했습니다. "야구 시즌이 시작되려면 아직 몇 달 남았는걸."

제크는 한숨을 쉬었고 고개를 가로저었습니다.

"내가 말하는 구멍이 열리는 날은 말이야." 그는 말했습니다. "야구와 아무런 상관이 없어. 그날은 네가 사는 우주와 내가 사는 우주 바로 서로의 옆으로 이동하는 때야. 그런 일은 자주 일어나지 않지. 그 일이 다시 일어나려면 몇 년은 걸릴 거야."

"일식이나 월식 같은 그런 거야?" 제가 물었습니다.

"그런 셈이지." 그가 말했습니다. "구멍이 열리는 날이 되면, 우리는 약장 같은, 어떤 구멍을 통해서 볼 수 있어. 그러면 우리는 너희의 우주를 볼 수 있는 거지. 그건, 그런데, 우리 우주보다 조금이라도 더 좋은 게 없어."

"우리 우주가 더 좋다고 난 말하지 않았어." 제가 말했습니다. "우리 우주가 더 좋다고 내가 말했니?"

"아마 안 했겠지. 그런데 틀림없이 너는 그렇게 생각하고 있었을 거야." 그가 말했습니다. "너희에게 있는 것은 우리

한테도 다 있어. 그리고 그건 그만큼 좋아, 내 말을 믿어. 어쩌면 훨씬 더 좋을걸."

"알았어, 알았다고!" 제가 말했습니다. 그러고 나서 저는 바닥에서 일어났습니다. 저는 제크의 욕실에서 처음으로 평행 우주를 자세히 살펴보았습니다.

흐으음.

그것은 제 욕실과 꽤 똑같아 보였습니다. 다만 좀 달랐습니다. 우선, 세면대에 특이한 것이 있었습니다. 거기에는 수도꼭지가 두 개 있었습니다. 그러나 그 수도꼭지에는 '찬물'과 '덜 찬물'이라고 표시되어 있었습니다.

그다음에 저는 변기 옆에 있는 화장지를 보았습니다. 그것은 사포처럼 생겼습니다. 저는 화장실을 사용해야 할 만큼 평행 우주에 오래 있지 않기를 바랐습니다.

저는 욕실 바닥에 물이 많다는 것을 알아차렸습니다. 제가 샤워기를 흘끗 보았을 때 저는 그 이유를 알았습니다. 샤워 커튼 대신에, 베니션 블라인드(venitian blind)가 있었습니다.

"그래, 뉴어욕은 어떤 곳이야?" 제가 물었습니다.

"아주 멋지지." 그가 말했습니다.

"TV 채널은 몇 개나 있어?" 제가 물었습니다.

그는 저를 수상쩍다는 듯이 바라보았습니다.

"너희는 채널이 하나 이상이야?" 그가 물었습니다.

"그만하자." 제가 대답했습니다.

"야." 그가 말했습니다. "빅 바나나(Big Banana)에 있는 모든 것은 네가 뉴욕에서 누릴 수 있는 그 어떤 것만큼이나 좋단 말이야."

"아, 너희는 뉴어욕을 빅 바나나라고 부르는구나." 제가 말했습니다. "우리가 뉴욕을 빅 애플(Big Apple)이라고 부르는 것처럼 말이야."

"바나나가 사과보다 훨씬 더 멋진 과일이지." 그가 말했습니다.

"이봐." 제가 말했습니다. "너희 우주에 있는 모든 것이 모든 면에서 우리 우주만큼 멋지다고 난 확신해, 알겠니? 이제 내 유지 장치를 받을 수 있을까? 그러고 나서 내가 되돌아가는 것 좀 도와줄래?"

"제크, 너 짐 싸고 있니?" 그 목소리는 우리 아빠의 목소리와 정말 비슷하게 들렸습니다.

"네, 아빠!" 제크가 대답했습니다.

"그래, 서둘러라! 택시는 8시에 올 거야."

저는 제크를 의심스럽게 쳐다보았습니다.

"너는 아빠랑 어디 갈 예정이니?" 제

가 물었습니다.

"응, 우리는 비행기를 타야 해."

저는 갑자기 어지러운 기분이 들었습니다.

"네 아빠가 혹시라도 너를 뉴욕 양키스 훈련 캠프에 데려가시는 건 아니지, 그렇지?" 제가 물었습니다.

"아니야."

"그래, 그거 다행이네." 제가 말했습니다.

"아빠는 뉴어욕 영키스(Newer York Yunkees)의 훈련 캠프에 나를 데려가실 거야. 뉴어욕 영키스는 트리플-A 마이너리그 팀이야. 그들은 양키스만큼이나 좋아."

"세상에." 저는 작은 소리로 말했습니다. "네 인생은 나와 똑같구나, 조금 다른 것 빼고 말이야, 그렇지 않니?"

"그럼, 당연하지!" 그가 말했습니다. "그게 바로 평행 우주라고 하는 거야, 잭." 그의 말은 4학년 학생에게 말하고 있는 것처럼 들렸습니다. 저는 그게 별로 마음에 들지 않았는데, 왜냐하면 저는 5학년이기 때문입니다. "사실을 알고 싶니? 나는 진짜가 아닌 복사판에 사는 것에 조금 질렸어."

"질렸다고? 그렇지만 네가 방금 말한 건—"

"내가 뭐라고 말했는지는 잊어버려. 나는 아마 평행 우주에 살 거야. 그런데

나는 바보가 아니거든. 내가 영키스 말고 양키스가 훈련하는 것을 더 보고 싶어한다고 생각하지 않아?"

"네가 뭐라고 하는지 안 들린다, 제크!" 그의 아빠가 말했습니다. "너 나에게 말하고 있니?"

"아니에요, 혼잣말이에요!" 그가 외쳤습니다. 그러고 나서 그는 저에게 말했습니다. "야, 나에게 좋은 생각이 났어. 우리가 장소를 바꿔 보는 게 어때? 내가 네 아빠와 함께 양키스의 훈련 캠프에 갈게. 너는 우리 아빠와 영키스의 캠프에 가는 거야."

"말도 안 돼." 제가 말했습니다.

"그럼 됐어." 그가 말했습니다. "나도 꼭 하고 싶었던 건 아니야."

"너 유지 장치를 아직 안 챙겼니?" 제크의 아빠가 외쳤습니다.

"걱정 마세요!" 제크는 불안한듯 대답했습니다.

"오 이런." 제가 말했습니다. "설마 너도 네 유지 장치를 찾을 수 없다는 건 아니겠지!"

"그게 어때서?" 그가 말했습니다.

이건 저를 정말 기겁하게 했습니다.

"제크야." 그의 아빠가 불렀습니다. 그가 문 바로 밖에서 말하는 것처럼 들렸습니다. "너 그 안에 있니?"

제크는 겁을 먹은 것 같았습니다.

"네가 여기 있는 것을 아빠가 보시면

안 돼." 그가 속삭였습니다. "너는 숨어야 해!"

"어디에?"

"여기."

그는 저를 욕조로 데리고 갔습니다. 그는 블라인드를 젖혀서 저를 안으로 밀어 넣었습니다. 그런 뒤 저는 그가 약장 문을 열고 닫는 소리를 들었습니다. 그다음에 아무 소리도 나지 않았습니다. 그는 무슨 일을 하려는 걸까요?

저는 제 손목시계를 보았습니다. 우리가 탈 택시가 오기 전까지 저에게는 겨우 30분이 남았습니다. 평행 우주에 있는 욕조 안에 숨어서 저는 무엇을 하고 있는 걸까요? 제가 사는 세상으로 저는 어떻게 돌아갈 수 있을까요?

저는 블라인드 틈새로 엿보았습니다. 제크는 어느 곳에서도 보이지 않았습니다. 그때 저는 깨달았습니다.

그 망할 녀석이 약장 문을 통해서 제 우주로 슬며시 빠져나간 것입니다!

5장

저는 겁에 질렸습니다.

바로 지금 이 순간, 제크는 제가 된 것처럼 굴고 있습니다. 그는 우리 아빠와 함께 플로리다에서 하는 양키스 훈련 캠프로 떠날 준비를 하고 있을 것입니다!

저는 욕실 문을 두드리는 소리를 들었습니다.

"제크, 내 말 들었니? 준비 다 됐어?" 그의 아빠의 목소리가 말했습니다.

저는 숨을 죽였습니다.

문이 열렸습니다. 제크의 아빠가 욕실 안으로 들어왔습니다. 바로 그때 저는 재채기를 했습니다.

"에이취!"

"제크? 너 샤워 중이니?"

"아니에요." 제가 대답했습니다.

블라인드가 위로 올라갔습니다. 우리 아빠와 거의 똑같이 생긴 아빠가 서 있었습니다.

처음에 저는 그가 화를 낼까 봐 겁에 질렸습니다. 그러나 그는 웃기 시작했습니다.

"너는 옷을 입은 채로 샤워실에서 뭘 하고 있니?" 그가 물었습니다.

"쉬고 있었어요." 제가 대답했습니다.

"쉴 시간이 없단다, 제크. 우리가 탈 택시가 30분 내로 올 거야. 네 유지 장치를 챙겼니? 짐은 다 쌌어?"

"거의요." 제가 말했습니다.

그는 저를 묘하게 쳐다보았고 인상을 썼습니다.

"너 좀 달라 보인다, 애야. 오늘 아침에 새로운 방향으로 머리를 빗었니?"

"네. 그랬어요. 그게 바로 제가 한 일

이에요."

"으음. 좋아. 자, 나는 아직 할 일이 몇 가지 남아 있단다. 제크, 너 세탁소에 빨리 가서 우리 세탁물을 다 찾아와 줄래?"

세탁소라니요! 제가 가고 싶은 유일한 곳은 약장을 통해 되돌아가는 것입니다. 그렇지만 제가 무슨 말을 할 수 있겠어요?

"어, 그–그래요." 저는 말을 더듬었습니다. "어느 세탁소인지 다시 말씀해 주실래요?"

"알잖아. 길 건너서 한 블록 아래에 있는 곳 말이다."

"으음. 그리고 어느 블록에 있었죠?"

그는 저를 쳐다보았고 눈썹을 치켜 올렸습니다.

"왜 이러니." 그가 말했습니다. "너 거기에 많이 가 봤잖아. 그냥 얼른 가. 우리는 곧 떠나야 해."

"알겠어요." 저는 말했습니다.

그는 저에게 영수증과 20달러 지폐를 건네주었습니다. 그러고 나서 그는 욕실 밖으로 걸어 나갔습니다.

그 20달러 지폐는 이상하게 생겼습니다. 그것은 아주 컸습니다. 그리고 제가 그것을 자세히 살펴보았을 때, 저는 지폐의 윗부분을 따라 "미분산국(The Untied States of America)"이라고 쓰여 있는 것을 보았습니다. 제가 봤던 모든

20달러 지폐에 들어간 그림에는 앤드루 잭슨(Andrew Jackson)이 있었습니다. 여기에는 텁수룩한 머리와, 턱수염을 기르고, 코안경을 낀 누군가의 그림이 있었습니다. 그의 이름은 슬래피 쿠퍼맨(Slappy Kupperman)이었습니다.

저는 아파트를 떠나서 엘리베이터를 타고 내려갔습니다. 그러고 나서 저는 밖으로 나갔습니다. 저는 할 수 있는 한 빨리 세탁소에 갔다가 돌아오고 싶었습니다.

길 모퉁이에서 저는 차들이 멈추기를 기다렸습니다. 시간이 정말 오래 걸리고 있었습니다. 그때 저는 신호등을 올려다 보았고 왜 그런지 알았습니다. 빨간 등과 녹색 등 대신에, 4개의 등이 있었습니다.

그 등에는 "**멈추세요**", "**아직 아닙니다**", "**기다리세요**", 그리고 "**좋아요, 어서 가세요**"라고 쓰여 있었습니다.

뉴어욕은 확실히 기묘한 곳이었습니다.

제 오른편에 있는 커다란 광고판에는 "**우리는 뉴어욕을 사랑해요! 뉴욕만큼 좋아요! 어쩌면 더 좋습니다!**"라고 써 있었습니다. 글쎄요, 저는 그렇게 생각하지 않았습니다. 저는 제 우주로 되돌아가고 싶었습니다.

저는 그 세탁소를 겨우 찾아냈습니다. 저는 제크 아빠의 옷을 받았습니다.

그리고 저는 그곳에서 서둘러 나왔습니다. 저는 그 블록을 따라서 되돌아갔습니다. 그러나 왜 그런지 몰라도 제가 틀림없이 실수한 것 같았습니다. 왜냐하면 제가 모퉁이에 도착했을 때, 그 커다란 광고판이 제 왼편에 있어야 했기 때문입니다. 하지만 거기에는 아무 것도 없었습니다.

저는 재빨리 주변을 돌아보았습니다. 어떤 것도 눈에 익은 것이 없었습니다. 그때 저는 길 건너편에 있는 커다란 아파트 건물을 보았습니다. 거기에는 화려한 차양이 있었습니다. 그것은 제가 사는 우주의 우리 동네에 있는 것과 아주 많이 비슷해 보였습니다. 비크먼 암즈 플라자 아파트(The Beekman Arms Plaza Apartments) 말이죠. 제가 제크의 집으로 돌아가는 길을 찾도록 그 건물의 경비원이 저를 도와줄 수도 있겠다고 생각했습니다. 문제는, 제크의 그 빌어먹을 주소를 제가 모른다는 것입니다. 제가 아는 것이라고는 그 주소도 아마 저의 집 주소와 비슷할 거라는 점입니다. 약간만 다르겠지요.

저는 그 건물로 달려갔습니다. 그러나 그곳에는 경비원이 한 명도 없었습니다. 사실, 그곳에는 심지어 그 어떤 건물도 없었습니다! 제가 건물이라고 생각했던 것은 영화 촬영 세트처럼, 그냥 가짜로 만든 정면 외관이었습니다. 그 앞에 있는 덤불은 녹색 플라스틱으로 만든 것이었습니다. 거기에는 꼬리표가 붙어 있었습니다. 거기에는 이렇게 쓰여 있었습니다. "진짜 같은 덤불. 오랫동안 유지됩니다. 관리가 덜 필요합니다. 진짜보다 좋아요."

저는 침을 꿀꺽 삼켰습니다. 저는 꿈 속에 있는 것처럼 느껴졌습니다. 어딘가로 가려고 아무리 애를 써도, 갈 수가 없어서, 결국은 토하게 되는, 그런 정말 끔찍한 꿈 가운데 하나 말입니다.

길 한복판에서 저는 뚜껑이 열려 있는 맨홀(manhole)을 보았습니다. 그 주변에는 경찰 방어벽이 있었습니다. 표지판에는 이렇게 쓰여 있었습니다. **"구멍이 열리는 날 주의! 구멍에 빠지는 것은 멍청한 일입니다! 또한 고통스럽습니다! 불법이라고 우리가 말했나요?"**

엇! 이것은 제 우주로 되돌아갈 수 있는 다른 방법이 될 수 있겠어요! 제크의 집으로 가는 길을 찾고 나서 약장을 통해 되돌아갈 수 없다면, 여기를 통해서 갈 수 있을지도 모릅니다. 당연히, 하수구를 통해서 가는 것은 정말 역겨울 거예요. 그렇지만 저는 신경 쓰지 않습니다. 적어도 제가 올바른 편으로 나가기만 한다면요.

저는 신호등이 바뀌기를 기다렸습니다. 이번에도 시간이 정말 오래 걸렸습니다. 그다음에 저는 맨홀 쪽으로 급히 달려갔습니다. 이제는 제가 움직일 시간이었습니다. 그러나 제가 막 허리를 굽혔을 때, 저는 제 어깨 위에 묵직한 손이 놓이는 것을 느꼈습니다.

저는 올려다보았습니다. 몸집이 큰 경찰관이 제 몸 너머로 서 있었습니다. 그는 좀 무섭게 생겼습니다. 그러나 곧 저는 그의 권총집에 있는 권총을 보았습니다. 그것은 슈퍼 소커(Super Soaker)였습니다.

"너무 가까이 다가서서 뉴욕으로 떨어지고 싶은 건 아니겠지." 그가 말했습니다. "그렇지, 애야?"

"오 이런, 아저씨. 저는 분명히 그러고 싶지 않아요." 제가 말했습니다.

제가 뉴욕으로 떨어지는 것처럼 바보 같은 일을 하고 싶어한다는 생각에 대해 우리 둘 다 한바탕 웃었습니다.

"자 그렇다면, 거기에서 물러서렴." 그가 말했습니다.

저는 그렇게 했습니다. 그는 맨홀 바로 옆에 계속 서 있었습니다. 저는 그가 저를 믿는다고 생각하지 않습니다. 그러나 슈퍼 소커를 가지고 있는, 그는 더 이상 그렇게 무서워 보이지 않았습니다. 저는 그에게 도움을 청하기로 결심했습니다.

"어, 경찰관 아저씨." 제가 말했습니다. "저는 길을 잃어버렸어요. 저는 집에 가는 길이었어요. 그런데 제가 다른 곳으로 방향을 잘못 틀었거나 뭐 그런 것 같아요."

"주소가 어떻게 되니, 꼬마야?"

"제 주소요?"

"그래."

"어, 그게, 저도 정확하게 모르겠어요." 제가 말했습니다. "제 말은 일시적으로 그것을 깜빡 잊은 것 같다는 말이에요."

"네 주소를 깜빡 잊었다고?"

"일시적으로요."

그는 저를 이상하다는 듯이 바라보았습니다. 그러나 그는 제가 제크가 사는 건물에 대해 설명하는 동안 제 말을 들어 주었습니다.

"아, 네가 말하는 곳을 알겠어." 그가 말했습니다. "내가 너를 그곳에 데려다 주마."

그는 제 손을 잡았습니다. 그러고 나서 그는 저를 데리고 블록을 따라 가서 모퉁이를 돌았습니다.

거기에, 제크가 사는 건물이 있었습니다! 저는 그에게 정신없이 감사 인사를 했고, 그다음에 저는 자리를 떠났습니다. 저를 보내서 그는 아마 기분이 좋았을 것입니다.

제크가 사는 건물 바로 앞에는 신문 판매대가 있었습니다. 제가 사는 건물 앞에 있는 것과 똑같았습니다. 모든 신문의 1면에는 다음과 같은 표제가 큰 글

씨로 쓰여 있었습니다.

"위험! 구멍이 열리는 날 도래! 위험한 시도를 하지 않도록 경고 받은 시민들"

위험하다고? 뭐가 위험하다는 걸까요? 저는 신문을 한 부 집어 들었고 읽기 시작했습니다.

"오늘, 이른 아침에, 뉴어욕의 시민들은 다시 한번 여러 구멍들 가운데 어느 곳을 통해서 들여다보고 우리 자매 우주의 생활을 실제로 관찰할 수 있게 되었다. '대체 우주로 넘어가려고 하지 마세요!'라고 뉴어욕 평행 우주 연구소의 롤런드 펜스터(Roland Fenster) 교수가 경고했다. '구멍들은 대략 오전 6시경에 열릴 것입니다. 그것들은 대략 두 시간 후에 다시 단단히 닫힐 것입니다. 일단 닫히면, 그것들은 30년 동안 다시 열리지 않을 것입니다. 30년이라는 시간은 우리보다 더 낫다고 잘못 소문이 났지만, 그렇지 않은 우주에서 보내기에 정말 길고 긴 시간입니다.'"

저는 제 손목시계를 보았습니다. 이크! 오전 7시 45분이었습니다. 택시가 와서 제크가 우리 아빠와 함께 플로리다로 떠나기 전까지 저에게 겨우 15분이 남아 있었습니다. 그리고 제 우주로 가는 문이 30년 동안 닫히기 전까지 말입니다!

저는 제크네 건물 안으로 달려 들어갔습니다.

6장

저는 숨을 헐떡거리며 제크의 아파트에 돌아왔습니다. 저는 현관에 제크 아빠의 세탁물을 떨어뜨렸습니다. 저는 욕실로 달려 들어갔습니다.

저는 약장 뒷부분을 세게 밀었습니다. 그러나 저는 그 망할 것을 조금도 움직이게 할 수 없었습니다. 제크는 분명 제가 알고 있는 것보다 우주 간 이동에 대해 더 많이 알고 있었습니다!

그리고 그때 저는 제 뒤에서 누군가의 소리를 들었습니다. 저는 돌아서서 제크의 아빠가 이상하게 저를 보고 있는 것을 발견했습니다.

"제크야." 그가 말했습니다. "너 뭐 하고 있니?"

그에게 사실을 말해야 할까요? 제가 그를 믿어도 될까요? 아니면 그는 적일까요? 저는 모릅니다. 그러나 시간이 얼마 남지 않았습니다. 그리고 저에게 선택의 여지가 많지 않다는 것을 알았습니다.

"들어 보세요, 아저씨." 저는 말했습니다. "이건 좀 의심스럽게 들리실 거예요. 그렇지만 사실이에요, 그러니 저 좀 도와주세요."

"좋아, 제크." 그가 말했습니다. "그렇지만 서둘러라. 택시가 오기 전까지 15분도 남지 않았단다."

"알겠어요." 제가 말했습니다. "먼저, 저는 아저씨의 아들, 제크가 아니에요. 저는 그 아이와 똑같이 생긴 다른 사람이에요. 그리고 제 이름은 잭이에요. 저는 평행 우주에 살아요. 제 아빠와 저는 양키스 훈련 캠프에 갈 준비를 하고 있었어요. 아저씨와 제크가 양키스 훈련 캠프에 갈 준비를 하고 있었던 것처럼 말이에요. 다만 제가 제 유지 장치를 약장을 통해서 떨어뜨렸어요. 제크가 자기 것을 잃어버렸듯이, 저도 제 것을 잃어버렸어요."

제크 아빠의 입이 떡 벌어졌습니다. 그는 그의 손으로 자기 이마를 탁 하고 쳤습니다.

"정말 믿―을 수 없어!" 그가 말했습니다.

"그렇지만, 사실이에요, 아저씨." 제가 말했습니다. "맹세해요."

"제크가 유지 장치를 잃어버렸다고?" 그는 멍한 목소리로 말했습니다. "그건 올해만 해도 지금까지 열 개째야."

우와! 제크는 저보다 훨씬 더 심각하네요!

"너는 그런 물건이 얼마나 하는지 알고 있니?" 그가 물었습니다.

"1,200달러 아니면 112달러요." 저는 재빨리 말했습니다. "그런데 아저씨는 제가 말한 다른 이야기는 못 들으셨어요?"

"그래, 그래, 그래. 물론 들었지." 그가 말했습니다. "네 이름은 잭이지. 너는 약장 반대편의 평행 우주에 살고 있고, 어쩌고, 저쩌고."

"제 말을 안 믿으시는 거죠, 그렇죠?" 제가 말했습니다.

"내가 왜 네 말을 안 믿겠니?" 그가 말했습니다. "뉴어욕에 사는 모든 사람들은 네가 살고 있는 우주에 대해 알고 있어. 그것은 대단한 비밀이나 그런 게 아니야. 그리고 어쨌거나, 네가 살고 있는 우주가 우리 우주보다 더 좋지 않단다."

맙소사, 이곳 사람들에게 이건 정말 민감한 주제군요!

"저는 우리 우주가 더 좋다고 말하지 않았어요." 제가 말했습니다. "저기요, 아저씨. 아저씨는 평행 우주에 대해 잘 아시는 것 같아요. 그러면 약장을 통해서 제 우주로 돌아가는 방법을 아실지도 모르겠네요. 제크가 방금 그랬던 것처럼요."

"제크가?" 그가 말했습니다. "걔가 넘어갔다고?"

저는 고개를 끄덕였습니다. 저는 이제야 제대로 제크 아빠의 관심을 끌었습니다.

"하지만 지금 거의 7시 50분이야!" 제크의 아빠는 자신의 이마를 다시 쳤습니다. "8시에 구멍이 열리는 날은 완전히 끝날 거야!"

"제 말이 그 말이에요, 아저씨." 제가 말했습니다. "그런 일이 일어난다면 저는 정말 절망적일 거예요. 제 말은, 제가 이곳에 사는 것을 좋아하지 않을 것이란 게 아니에요. 왜냐하면 저는 이곳이 적어도 제가 사는 우주만큼이나 좋다고 생각하거든요. 그리고 어쩌면 더 좋을지도 몰라요. 하지만 요점은, 제가 정말로 우리 엄마 아빠를 보고 싶어 할 것이라는 거예요."

"알겠다, 알겠어." 제크의 아빠가 말했습니다. "네가 해야 하는 일은 바로 이거야. 네 손을 약장 뒷벽에 올려 놓으렴."

저는 그렇게 했습니다.

"눈을 감아라. 심호흡을 해. 이제 뒷벽이 열리는 것을 마음에 그려 보렴. 어떤 것이라도 느껴지면 나에게 말해 줘."

저는 그가 저에게 말한 것을 모두 했습니다. 효과가 생기기 시작했습니다. 뒷벽이 튀어 오르는 것처럼 느껴지기 시작했습니다. 저는 때마침 두 눈을 떠서 벽이 서서히 사라지는 것을 보았습니다.

7장

"안녕, 잭." 낯익은 얼굴이 말했습니다.

"제크!" 제크의 아빠가 말했습니다.

"오, 정말 다행이야!"

"제크!" 제가 말했습니다. "넌 돌아오고 있었어?"

그는 당황한 것 같았습니다.

"난 향수병에 걸렸어." 그가 말했습니다. "내 말은, 네 아빠는 정말 멋진 분이셔, 잭. 정말이야. 그런데 그는 우리 아빠가 아니잖아. 그리고 여기는 내 우주도 아니고. 너도 분명 똑같이 느끼고 있을 거라고 나는 생각했어. 뉴어욕이 뉴욕만큼이나 멋지다고 해도 말이야."

제 아빠가 약장의 반대편에 나타났습니다.

"아빠!" 제가 말했습니다.

"안녕, 잭." 제 아빠가 말했습니다. 그러고 나서 그는 제크의 아빠 쪽으로 돌아섰습니다. "안녕, 돈(Don)." 그가 말했습니다. "오랜만이군."

"안녕, 댄(Dan)." 제크의 아빠가 아빠에게 말했습니다.

그들은 약장을 통해서 서로 악수를 나누었습니다.

"두 분 서로 *아세요*?" 놀라서, 저는 물었습니다.

"그래. 우리가 너희 나이였을 때 만났어." 제크의 아빠가 말했습니다. "그렇지만 약장을 통해서 만난 것은 아니었어. 그건 빨래방의 건조기를 통해서였지."

"맞아." 우리 아빠가 말했습니다. "빨래를 하다가 한 짝이 없어지는 양말에 무슨 일이 일어난 건지 난 항상 궁금했거든. 그 양말들이 평행 우주로 간다고 누가 짐작이나 했겠니?"

"그날도 참 대단한 구멍이 열리는 날이었지." 제크의 아빠가 말했습니다. "빨래는 많이 못 말렸지만. 우리는 정말 즐거웠었지. 네 아빠는 내가 건조기 안에서 사는 줄 알았단다."

아빠와 제크의 아빠 모두 큰 소리로 웃었습니다.

"어, 끼어들어서 죄송한데요." 제가 말했습니다. "이건 정말 재미있는 일이에요. 그런데 지금 7시 55분이에요."

"오, 그렇지, 맞아!" 제크의 아빠가 말했습니다. 그는 약장을 통해 제크를 보았습니다. "얘야, 너 여전히 영키스 훈련 캠프에 가고 싶니?"

"당연히 가고 싶죠!" 제크가 말했습니다.

"그렇다면 내가 너를 끌어당겨 줄게." 제크의 아빠가 말했습니다.

그렇게 제크는 그의 우주로 기어서 돌아갔습니다. 저도 저의 우주로 기어서 돌아왔습니다.

"미안해, 잭." 제크가 말했습니다. "난 완전 얼간이였어."

"맞아." 제가 말했습니다. "그렇지만 용서할게."

택시의 경적 소리가 이제 약장의 양쪽 모든 곳에서 울리고 있었습니다.

"자, 잘 가요, 모두들." 제가 말했습니다.

"언젠가 또 만나." 제크가 말했습니다.

"아마도 다음 번 구멍이 열리는 날에 말이야." 제가 말했습니다.

"좋아." 제크가 말했습니다.

그는 자신의 주머니에서 뭔가를 끄집어냈습니다. 그는 약장을 통해서 그것을 저에게 건네주었습니다. 그것은 제 유지 장치였습니다!

"너 내 유지 장치를 슬쩍했니?" 제가 물었습니다.

그는 멋쩍어하며 고개를 끄덕였습니다.

"그렇지만 나는 그걸 가지고 있을 수는 없었어." 그가 말했습니다.

"왜냐하면 너는 그게 잘못된 일이라는 걸 아니까."

"맞아." 그가 말했습니다. "게다가 그건 맞지도 않았어."

그때 갑자기, 우리집 현관에 있는 큰 괘종시계가 울리기 시작했습니다.

8시였습니다.

우리는 손을 흔들며 서로에게 작별인사를 했습니다. 그다음에, 제크와 그의 아빠 얼굴을 마주보는 대신에, 저는 치약과 데오도런트(deodorant)가 있는 선반을 보고 있었습니다. 저는 약장 뒷벽을 힘껏 밀어 보았습니다. 저는 미친

듯이 마음속으로 그려 보았습니다. 그러나 아무 일도 일어나지 않았습니다.

이렇게 해서 저는 평행 우주를 발견하게 되었습니다. 그리고 제가 약장 문을 열 때마다, 저는 제크와 그의 아빠를 생각합니다. 저는 그들이 약간 그립습니다. 그들이 그렇게 가까이에 있으면서도, 그토록 멀리 있다고 생각하면 흥미롭습니다.

다음에 제크를 만날 때면, 저에게도 제 아들이 있겠지요. 이상해요! 그가 어떻게 생겼을지 궁금합니다. 와, 그가 저와 똑같이 생겼다면 멋지지 않을까요? 한 가지만 제외하고 모든 면에서 말이에요: 저는 그가 절대로 교정기를 착용할 필요가 없기를 바랍니다!

Chapter 1

1. D I always thought my building was normal, at least until the thing I'm about to tell you happened.

2. C My dad arranged to take me down to Florida. We were going to visit the New York Yankees at their spring training camp. My parents are divorced. Part of the time I live with my dad. He's a writer, and he gets to do lots of cool things. Like go to spring training and then write about it in a magazine.

3. A I was so excited, I woke up at about 6:00 A.M. The minute I opened my eyes, I realized something. I had forgotten to put my retainer in my mouth before I went to sleep.

4. B I left one retainer in a pair of jeans, which went in the laundry. It melted to the inside of the pocket. One got chewed up in my Grandma Leah's garbage disposal.

5. D I was sure my retainer was in the medicine cabinet in the bathroom, instead of in my mouth, where it should have been.

Chapter 2

1. B But maybe Mrs. Taradash had a grandson. Maybe her grandson looked almost exactly like me. And maybe her medicine cabinet was hooked up to ours on the other side.

2. B Mrs. Taradash looked at me like I was cuckoo. "I don't have a grandson, precious," she said.

3. A "If I let you look," she said, "will you go away and let me get back to sleep?" "Yes, ma'am," I said. She sighed a deep sigh. Then she waved me into the apartment.

4. D Weird. Everywhere you looked, there were stuffed animals. And I don't mean cuddly teddy bears, either. I mean real dead animals that were stuffed by a taxidermist.

5. C I hurried into the bathroom and looked around. There was no retainer on the floor or anywhere else. I opened the medicine cabinet. I pushed against the back. It didn't budge. So I closed the medicine cabinet door.

Chapter 3

1. C He really did look a whole lot like me. Only his teeth were a lot more crooked.

2. D "You don't live next door," I said. "Do you?" He shook his head. "Then where do you live?" "Someplace else. Someplace nearby, but kind of far away, too. Someplace you might think is weird."

3. B He suddenly tried to slam the door. But I was too fast for him. I stuck my arm into the medicine cabinet. That stopped him from shutting it.

4. A I grabbed his wrist. "Let go!" he shouted. "Not till you give me my retainer!"

5. B "Now you've really done it!" He looked frightened. "Done what?" I asked. "The one thing nobody is ever supposed to do," he said. "What's that?" I asked. "Cross over into a parallel universe!"

Chapter 4

1. D "The kind of Opening Day I'm talking about," he said, "has nothing to do with baseball. It's when your universe and mine move right next to each other. It doesn't happen a lot. It'll be years before it happens again."

2. B "Zeke, are you packing?" The voice sounded a lot like my dad's. "Yeah, Dad!" Zeke called back. "Well, hurry up! The cab is coming at 8:00." I looked at Zeke strangely. "You're going somewhere with your dad?" I asked. "Yeah. We have to catch a plane."

3. D "Oh my gosh," I said softly. "Your life is just the same as mine, except a little different, isn't it?" "Well, duh!" he said.

4. A "You want to know the truth? I'm a little tired of living in the one that's the copy and not the one that's the original." "You are? But you just said—" "Never mind what I said. I may live in a parallel universe. But I'm not stupid. Don't you think I'd rather be going to see the Yankees train than the Yunkees?"

"I can't hear you, Zeke!" called his dad. "Are you talking to me?" "No, to myself!" he shouted. Then to me he said, "Hey, I've got an idea. Why don't we switch places? I'll go to the Yankees' training camp with your dad. You can go to the Yunkees' with mine."

5. D "Zeke," called his dad. He sounded like he was right outside the door. "Are you in there?" Zeke looked scared. "We can't let him see you here," he whispered. "You've got to hide!" "Where?" "Here." He led me to the bathtub.

Chapter 5

1. C "Uh huh. OK. Well, I still have a few things to do. Zeke, could you run to the dry cleaners quickly and pick up all our cleaning?"

2. A A big billboard to my right said, "WE LOVE NEWER YORK! JUST AS GOOD AS NEW YORK. MAYBE BETTER!"

3. B In the middle of the street I saw an open manhole. There were police barricades around it. Signs said, "DANGER ON OPENING DAYS! FALLING IN WOULD BE STUPID! ALSO PAINFUL! DID WE MENTION ILLEGAL?" Hey! This could be another way to get back to my universe! If I couldn't find my way back to Zeke's and go through the medicine cabinet, maybe I could climb through here.

4. D He stayed right next to the manhole. I don't think he trusted me. But with his Super Soaker he didn't seem so scary anymore. I decided to ask his help.

5. A On the front page of all the newspapers were big headlines: "DANGER! OPENING DAY ARRIVES! CITIZENS WARNED NOT TO TAKE CHANCES!" Danger? What danger? I picked up a paper and started to read. "Today, in the early hours of the morning, citizens of Newer York will once again be able to peek through any of several openings and actually observe life in our sister universe. 'Do not attempt to cross over into the alternate universe!' warns Professor Roland Fenster at the Newer York Institute of Parallel Universes. 'The openings should appear somewhere in the vicinity of 6:00 A.M. They will then shut down tight again approximately two hours later.'"

Chapter 6

1. A Should I tell him the truth? Could I trust him? Or was he the enemy? I didn't know. But time was running out. And I didn't see that I had much choice.

2. C "I can't be-lieve it!" he said. "It's true, though, sir," I said. "I swear." "Zeke has lost his retainer?" he said in a dazed voice. "That's the tenth one so far this year."

3. C "Why shouldn't I believe you?" he said. "Everybody in Newer York knows about your universe. It's not like it's a big secret or anything."

4. B "But it's almost 7:50!" Zeke's dad smacked his forehead again. "At 8:00 Opening Day will shut down completely!" "My point exactly, sir," I said. "I'd be miserable if that happened. Not that I wouldn't love living here, I mean. Because I think it's at least as good as my universe. And maybe even better. But the thing is, I'd really miss my mom and dad." "OK, OK," said Zeke's dad. "This is what you have to do. Put your hand on the back wall of the medicine cabinet."

5. D "This is what you have to do. Put your hand on the back wall of the medicine cabinet." I did. "Close your eyes. Take a deep breath. Now visualize the back wall opening."

Chapter 7

1. B "I got homesick," he said. "I mean, your dad is awfully nice, Zack. He really is. But he's not my dad. And this isn't my universe."

2. C "Hi, Zack," said my dad. Then he turned to Zeke's dad. "Hi, Don," he said. "Long time, no see." "Hi, Dan," said Zeke's dad to my dad. They shook hands through the medicine cabinet.

3. D "You two know each other?" I asked, amazed. "Yeah, we met when we were your age," said Zeke's dad. "But it wasn't through a medicine cabinet. It was through a dryer in the laundromat."

4. A "OK," said Zeke. He fished something out of his pocket. He handed it to

me through the cabinet. It was my retainer! "You swiped my retainer?" I said. He nodded sheepishly.

5. B So that's how I discovered the parallel universe. And every time I open my medicine cabinet, I think of Zeke and his dad. I kind of miss them. It's funny to think that they're so close, and yet so far away.

거울장 나라의 잭
(Through The Medicine Cabinet)

1판 1쇄   2020년 1월 10일
2판 1쇄   2024년 10월 21일

지은이   Dan Greenburg
기획   이수영
책임편집   정소이 배주윤
콘텐츠제작및감수   롱테일 교육 연구소
저작권   명채린
마케팅   두잉글 사업 본부

펴낸이   이수영
펴낸곳   롱테일북스
출판등록   제2015-000191호
주소   04033 서울특별시 마포구 양화로 113, 3층(서교동, 순흥빌딩)
전자메일   help@ltinc.net

ISBN 979-11-93992-35-7 14740